A HISTORY OF REPEATED INJURIES

A HISTORY OF REPEATED INJURIES

Threats to Liberty Since American Independence

EDITED BY THOMAS A. BERRY

CATO INSTITUTE

Hardcover ISBN: 978-1-969284-06-9
eBook ISBN: 978-1-969284-07-6

Chapter 1, revised and updated, is reprinted from *Limiting Leviathan*, ed. Donald P. Racheter and Richard E. Wagner (Edward Elgar Publishing, 1999). It was also reprinted in 1999 in *Cato's Letters* (#13), a series of distinguished essays on political economy and public policy published by the Cato Institute.

Cover: Faceout Studio, Addie Lutzo.

Library of Congress Control Number: 2026930461
Printed in the United States of America.

CATO
INSTITUTE
1000 Massachusetts Ave. NW
Washington, DC 20001

www.cato.org

CONTENTS

INTRODUCTION

THOMAS A. BERRY

Two hundred fifty years ago, the 13 colonies unanimously declared their independence from the kingdom of Great Britain and their new identity as the 13 United States of America. Taking such a drastic step meant the American Founders had to make the case for the necessity of their actions. So, in the Declaration of Independence, Thomas Jefferson laid out that case. He recounted, succinctly and methodically, "a history of repeated injuries and usurpations" at the hands of the king. The Declaration lists, point by point, "a long train of abuses and usurpations." Jefferson aimed to establish a pattern, demonstrating that Great Britain had "a design to reduce" the residents of the American colonies "under absolute Despotism." Put plainly, the king had the "direct object" of "the establishment of an absolute Tyranny over these States."

Of course, the story has a happy ending. Two hundred fifty years later, America is still independent and no longer under the control of any king. We live under a constitution, written just 11 years after the Declaration, that was designed purposefully to avoid many of the worst tyrannies that the colonies suffered.

In this volume, we explore a simple but profound question: 250 years later, how successful have we been? Are we entirely free of the "injuries and usurpations" the Framers complained of? Or have modern analogues of old tyrannies crept into our own government, leading to losses of liberty akin to those the colonists suffered?

Each chapter in this volume is centered on one of the injuries (or categories of injuries) listed in the Declaration. In each chapter, the author will connect the history of the Founding era with modern history, framed by one or more passages from the Declaration's list of grievances. The aim is to put the language of the Declaration in greater context, looking both backward and forward. What led Thomas Jefferson to include a particular line in the Declaration, and what challenges do we face now that most closely echo that history?

> "We hold these truths to be self-evident, that all men are created equal, that they are endowed by their Creator with certain unalienable Rights, that among these are Life, Liberty and the pursuit of Happiness."

Roger Pilon, the founding director of the Cato Institute's Center for Constitutional Studies, kicks off the volume with an explanation of the philosophical underpinnings of the Declaration. As Pilon explains, the Declaration is crucial to understanding the Framers' philosophy of government, a philosophy that would greatly influence the drafting of the Constitution 11 years later. "In a few brief lines, penned near the start of our struggle to secure our independence, the Founders distilled their philosophy of government: equal liberty for all, defined by rights to life, liberty, and the pursuit of happiness, secured by a government instituted for that purpose, its limited powers derived from the consent of the governed."

> "He has endeavoured to prevent the population of these States; for that purpose obstructing the Laws for Naturalization of Foreigners; refusing to pass others to encourage their migrations hither, and raising the conditions of new Appropriations of Lands."

David Bier, Cato's director of immigration studies, writes on the past and present of immigration restrictionism. As Bier explains, "Free immigration was a central principle for the Founders." Thomas Jefferson himself had written, prior to the Declaration, that emigration was "a right which nature has given to all men, of departing from the country in which chance, not choice, has placed them, of going in quest of new habitations."[1] And during the Constitutional Convention, Benjamin Franklin urged that the new Constitution should not "discourage the common people from removing to this Country."[2] Indeed, as Bier sums up, "The Founders were so universally in favor of free immigration that their primary debates were focused on how much to encourage it."

And these attitudes bore tremendous fruit. "The Founders' immigration policy was possibly the most successful economic policy ever adopted in American history. Allowing free immigration facilitated legal entry and population growth on an unprecedented scale, which generated enormous economic growth and prosperity." Yet for the last century, America has turned away from this tradition. "Before the immigration acts in the 1920s, people were presumed eligible to immigrate to the United States, and the government had to prove that they fell into an ineligible category, such as being a criminal. Since 1924, the presumption has flipped. Now, all immigrants are presumed ineligible *unless* they prove they fall into an exception." It remains to be seen whether America will return to the welcoming approach embraced by the Framers.

"For imposing Taxes on us without our Consent"

Adam N. Michel, Cato's director of tax policy studies, writes on the history of American taxation with Joshua Loucks, Cato research associate. As they explain, "The American Revolution was a tax revolt over consent; but it was also a rebellion against a system of taxation that was punitive, discriminatory, and enriching special interests on the other side of the Atlantic." If the taxes imposed by the British "hadn't been arbitrary, punitive, and discriminatory, a revolt over consent may never have happened." That is why "structural protections such as the apportionment requirement for direct taxes and the uniformity clause for indirect taxes were written into the Constitution to guard against regional favoritism and economic oppression."

But today, our system of taxation looks very different from what the Framers envisioned. As Michel and Loucks observe, "the introduction of the federal income tax in 1913 marked a turning point, fundamentally changing how Americans are taxed." Today, "while the overall tax burden is considerably higher than it was in the Founding era, federal taxes fall disproportionately on higher earners, while a growing share of the population pays little or nothing." Unequal treatment under the tax system breeds resentment, as it did in 1913. Many Americans "remain dissatisfied with the fiscal system for the same two reasons the Founding Generation gave: The overall fiscal burden has grown significantly, hindering wealth-building and independence, and the tax system has become a tool of political favoritism."

> "He has kept among us, in Times of Peace, Standing Armies without the Consent of our legislatures.
>
> He has affected to render the Military independent of and superior to the Civil power."

Brandan Buck, a research fellow in foreign policy studies at Cato, writes on the history of standing armies and conscription in America. Buck recounts a long tradition of "opponents of American militarism" who "believed that the creation of a large standing army, particularly via conscription, fundamentally altered the individual's relationship to the state, while corroding civil liberties and the domestic economy."

But as Buck explains, "the Second World War and its related political realignments contained and eventually strangled the final voices of opposition to the increasing role of the military in society and its effect on American civil liberties." Many policymakers "saw the Korean War and the greater Cold War as a crisis that demanded the United States rethink its traditional reluctance to maintaining a large peacetime military." But this history is not all bad news; the draft was abolished in 1973, after sustained advocacy "fed in no small part by a nascent libertarian movement."

> "For cutting off our Trade with all Parts of the World"

Dartmouth economics professor Douglas A. Irwin writes on the history of trade restrictionism. As Irwin recounts, "controversy about authority over trade policy was bound up with the demands for political independence at the very start of the country." Trade has always been central to the American economy: "For more than a century after the first permanent English settlement in North America was established at Jamestown in 1607, the New World settlers were heavily dependent on foreign trade." Indeed, an important event on the path to independence was when the British Parliament asserted "full power and authority to make laws and govern the colonies and reiterated its legal right to tax both external and internal commerce." As this history shows, modern disputes over tariffs and trade policy echo analogous disputes from centuries earlier.

"He has dissolved Representative Houses repeatedly for opposing with manly Firmness his Invasions on the Rights of the People."

Brent Skorup, legal fellow in Cato's Robert A. Levy Center for Constitutional Studies, writes on the history of executive orders issued unilaterally by American presidents. Although the Declaration was intended to bring the then-nascent United States out from under the tyranny of a king, all too often presidents have acted unilaterally to impose their will in king-like fashion, bypassing Congress. As Skorup explains, "modern presidents have exercised immense discretion that often functions identically to—and even displaces—lawmaking by Congress." These executive orders "are powerful, and they appeal to presidents largely because their issuance is not constrained by bicameralism, presentment, and constraints on administrative agencies like the Administrative Procedure Act." And all too often, their legality rests on shaky ground. "Time and again, vague statutory references and unspecified constitutional powers cited in executive orders have been used to justify sweeping assertions of government power into Americans' lives, livelihoods, and property."

"For depriving us in many Cases, of the Benefits of Trial by Jury"

Clark Neily, Cato's senior vice president for legal studies, writes on how plea bargaining and mass adjudication have drastically reduced the strength of the criminal jury right. As Neily notes, "Among the most readily abused powers of government is the ability to accuse someone of a crime and then prosecute, convict, and punish that person. Indeed, throughout history, the ability to initiate criminal prosecutions and impose punishments with the imprimatur of judicial legitimacy has been among the effective tools used by repressive regimes against perceived dissidents." But through the rise of plea bargaining and other tactics, juries "are now practically extinct on American soil. As a result, and utterly contrary to the Framers' design, ordinary citizens have virtually no personal involvement in the administration of criminal justice." The Framers enshrined the jury trial right in the Constitution because they were well aware of how easily criminal law can be abused. "British kings and queens generally preferred to operate within the ambit of formal law by enlisting the legislative authority of Parliament and creating special adjudicative bodies like the Star Chamber to provide legal cover for their predations." Unfortunately, we now find ourselves in a system in which there is hardly ever accountability when modern prosecutors similarly abuse the criminal justice system.

In addition, I write on the parallel weakening of the *civil* jury right. "Americans were well aware of the tactics that government officials might use to avoid facing juries. In the years leading up to the Revolution, English colonial administrators attempted to subvert the right to a civil jury trial by trying cases in specialized courts called 'vice-admiralty' courts. Colonial authorities would seize American ships under the pretext that they had violated customs and revenue measures and then try their cases in the vice-admiralty courts, without the benefit of a jury." Today, federal agencies punish Americans through agency adjudication procedures rather than through jury trials. In these adjudications, "the deck is stacked heavily against the respondent from start to finish, with the burden of proof, as in the vice-admiralty courts of yore, effectively on the respondent rather than the government." Fortunately, however, it appears that the Supreme Court is trending toward once again protecting the jury trial right where agencies aim to impose civil punishments for alleged wrongdoing.

We hope that this volume will give a broad overview of where we started as a nation, where we are now, and how far we still have to go to achieve the visions of liberty and good government envisioned by those who bravely signed the Declaration of Independence 250 years ago.

Notes

1. Thomas Jefferson, "Thomas Jefferson, A Summary View of the Rights of British America," July 1774.
2. "Madison Debates," August 10, 1787, The Avalon Project, Yale Law School Lillian Goldman Law Library.

1

THE PURPOSE AND LIMITS OF GOVERNMENT

ROGER PILON

When America's Founders declared our independence from English rule in 1776, they did so through a document that has inspired countless millions around the world ever since: our Declaration of Independence. Written from "a decent Respect to the Opinions of Mankind," the Declaration set forth not only the immediate causes that impelled our political separation but a moral, political, legal, and economic vision that spoke to the ages. In a few brief lines, penned near the start of our struggle to secure our independence, the Founders distilled their philosophy of government: equal liberty for all, defined by rights to life, liberty, and the pursuit of happiness, secured by a government instituted for that purpose, its limited powers derived from the consent of the governed.

Yet today, too many Americans have lost touch with those principles and the ways they secure our freedom. Indeed, we have imposed on ourselves many of the abuses that drove the Founders to revolution. We are not alone in that, of course. Around the world today, even where the people purport to rule, we see expanding, largely unaccountable governments limiting liberty and trampling rights. As the

21st century's authoritarianism grows, we are thus called once again to breathe life into the foundational principles that have ever defined us as a people.

As we revisit our country's Founding principles in this volume, it will be crucial to learn from the experience of the past 250 years. For in setting forth their vision, the Founders sought not only to show how far English rule had strayed from that ideal, but more importantly, to lay a foundation for the legitimate but limited government they would soon seek for America. To a substantial extent they succeeded in that, for in the grand sweep of human events, America has fared rather better than many other nations that have also sought, in their own ways, to both authorize and limit new governments. We would be remiss, however, if we concluded from the Founders' relative success that their plan has worked as intended. In fact, it would take but a cursory reading of their writings to reveal that they intended nothing like our present American leviathan. Indeed, and again, many of the grievances the Declaration lists are today the ordinary stuff of American governments. It would surely pain those who pledged their lives, their fortunes, and their sacred honor to see how far we have strayed from the vision that so animated them.

With the aid of experience, then, this chapter will focus in particular on the theory underpinning the Declaration's universal insights, the moral order the Declaration sets out, and the place of government within that order. We will conclude, briefly, by showing how the Constitution, as completed by the Civil War Amendments, reflects those principles, yet how it has been undermined since then. Thus, our concern throughout is with that most basic of political ideals: legitimacy.[1] That was the main moral concern of the Founders as well, which the Declaration captures in but a single elegantly crafted line: "That to secure these Rights, Governments are instituted among Men, deriving their just Powers from the Consent of the Governed." Reason and consent, the two traditional sources of political legitimacy, are there joined for "a candid World" to see. It is for us today to see more clearly how they go together to both authorize and limit government, lending it a substantial measure of legitimacy in the process. Once we do, and once we see, toward the end of this chapter, what has become of the Founders' vision, we will be in a better position to begin restoring the design they so carefully crafted.

The Declaration of Independence

As the Founders undertook their work, their immediate aim, as noted, was to justify their decision to declare our independence from England's distant rule, which they did by setting forth a theory of legitimate government, then demonstrating how English rule had grown distant from and abusive of that ideal. In outlining their theory of legitimacy, however, they could hardly have begun with government, for the whole point was to show how a legitimate government with legitimate powers might come about legitimately, not to assume government's existence and legitimacy from the start. Had they begun their argument with government already in place, they would have begged the very question they set out to address. They would have argued in a circle.

From the outset, therefore, the Founders were engaged in a tradition of moral and political thought that has come to be called "state-of-nature theory." Reasoning in that tradition begins by positing a theoretical "state of nature," a state of affairs we today call "civil society," where society and social intercourse of all kinds obtain, but questions about the need and justification for government and about its proper role remain to be answered.[2]

Thus, in the Declaration's famous second paragraph, the argument falls quite naturally into two parts. First, starting with the individual, and appealing to reason, the Founders sketched the moral order in such a world as described by rights and correlative obligations. Second, they drew forth the political conclusions implicit in that moral order. Thus, the first few lines in that paragraph make no mention of government; that comes only after the moral order has been outlined. Accordingly, the first concern is to determine whether, in this civil society, we have rights against each other and, if so, what those rights might be. Only then will we be in a position to determine whether a government might be necessary to secure those rights, which include what rights we might have to bring a government into being, what rights or powers we might legitimately grant that government, and what rights we may have against it. Thus the justificatory strategy of state-of-nature theory.

"We hold these Truths to be self-evident"

It is crucial, therefore, to recognize that the Declaration's fundamental principles are grounded not in human will but in reason. Moreover, they are asserted not simply as "truths" but as "self-evident" truths, obvious immutable truths accessible through ordinary human reasoning.[3] Thus, from the start, America has rested on the long tradition of natural law—more precisely, on the natural rights branch of that tradition, which emerged from the Enlightenment, about which more below.[4] Standing opposed to moral skepticism, which holds that there are no moral truths or if there are we cannot know them; to moral dogmatism, which asserts all manner of often inconsistent, unjustifiable rights; and to legal positivism, which simply posits rights as reflecting the will of a sovereign, the Founders held, at the deepest level, that those self-evident truths were apodictic—unable to be rationally denied.

Notice, then, how the Founders' understanding of these self-evident truths was modest, yet, ironically, profound. They were skeptics, to be sure—skeptics of governmental power. But unlike many natural law theorists before and after them, to say nothing of modern welfare state advocates, they were focused not on any capacious "morals" claims, much less on today's "entitlements," but on liberty—liberty as a fundamental moral principle. They believed, quite simply, that there is a higher law of right and wrong from which to derive the positive law and against which to judge that law at any point in time. And at bottom, that higher law is the law of individual liberty—and individual responsibility.[5]

"that all Men are created equal"

Substantively, the argument begins with a premise about moral equality, defined immediately thereafter by our unalienable rights to life, liberty, and the pursuit of happiness. By thus defining the limited sense in which we are all created equal, the Founders clearly meant that we are all equal only, but crucially, in the sense that we all have equal natural rights—that no one has such rights superior to those of anyone else. Surely, the Founders could not have meant that we are otherwise equal, whatever that might mean. Nor could they have meant to imply that we can restrict liberty to promote equality—that our natural rights include the kinds of egalitarian "rights" the modern welfare state has created, which are purchased only at the expense of others' rights to liberty. For such rights would undercut the equal freedom that enables each of us, with our myriad differences, to flourish freely as we work our way through life.[6]

But if the premise of equality was not meant to imply modern egalitarianism, neither was it meant, as many in the natural law tradition have urged, to enable some to impose contested "morals" on others. If we are all equal in the limited but crucial sense that we all have equal natural rights to chart our own courses by our own lights, free from the interference of others, then we cannot be compelled to conform to the morality of others, however "superior" the views of those others might be as derived from a variety of subjective values. The only proviso is that, as we plan and live our lives, we respect the equal rights of others to do the same. A corollary of the premise of equality, of course, is equality before the law, a phrase that well captures the sense in which the Founders saw us all as equal, their actual practices aside. (In fact, in all that follows we must be careful to distinguish the Declaration's principles—our main concern—from the Founders' or our own adherence to those principles. Too often, as imperfect people, we have failed in that.)

"that they are endowed by their Creator with certain unalienable Rights"

As we move now from the Declaration's premise of equality to the self-evident truths that purportedly follow, we are challenged to reflect on the source of our natural rights—and, indeed, on the fundamental question of whether we even have such rights. Those are not idle questions, for over the years, many have argued that the Declaration's claims are not true, much less "self-evidently" true. This is not the place for a deep dive into the epistemological foundations of the Founders' vision—into questions about how we know that we have natural rights and how we can demonstrate that—but a brief outline of an answer is in order.

In the Declaration's first paragraph, the Founders had invoked "the Laws of Nature and of Nature's God" as justifying our independence. Here, in the second paragraph, they invoke a "Creator" who "endows" us with "certain unalienable Rights." Although history and prudence suggest that the Founders were employing ideas that resonated both with themselves and with those on behalf of whom they were speaking, sound justification requires more, especially in today's more secular world. In particular, it requires that we avoid a narrow, theocratic reading of those passages, one that implies, for example, that we have natural rights only because our Creator has endowed us with them. For again, that would amount to a circular argument, to simply positing a Creator rather than, say, a king or a parliament as the source of such rights.

Better it would be to begin not by asking about the source of our rights but rather by analyzing the essential character and operation of rights. At bottom, rights are adversarial relationships. To have a right is to have a justified claim against another such that that other has a correlative obligation to do or not do some particular thing.[7] But we don't normally assert our rights. We do so only if interfered with, in which case we "naturally," if only tacitly, demand a justification for the interference: "What are you doing? By what right do you interfere with my freedom?" If the other's justification fails, and he withdraws his claim, the prior status quo of equal freedom is restored. But if his claim against us is justified, and we act as thus obligated to, so also is an earlier status quo of equal freedom secured. Thus is the right to freedom "natural" and shown to be so by the pattern of behavior that naturally follows from interference. (More on this below.) And thus the importance of the Declaration's premise, its benchmark of equal liberty.[8]

Instead of reading the Declaration's line invoking a Creator narrowly, therefore, as the "source" of our rights—our "God-given" rights as is often said—it would be far sounder, logically, to draw out the line's deeper meaning and read it as asserting, at bottom, the universality of natural rights, quite apart from religious beliefs of whatever kind. Indeed, given that the Founders themselves held various religious beliefs; given that they were devoted to liberty, and to religious liberty in particular; and given, especially, that they were asserting universal principles and universal rights common to all humans, believers and nonbelievers alike, we should understand that they were deriving our natural rights through universal human reasoning and behavior, common to all, rather than through often disputed theological beliefs, the better to avoid undermining the universality they surely meant to convey.

Implicit in this passage, however, is a corollary of the greatest importance. For if human reasoning can demonstrate that we all have natural rights, then we do not get those rights from government; in fact, whatever rights or powers government has, as the Declaration goes on to say, are given to it by us. Indeed, where would government get its powers if not from the people? For the people create government and hence come before it. Both logically and temporally, therefore, people and their natural rights come first, government second, as a means to secure those rights.

Thus, we are not servants of government, beholden to it for our rights; rather, government is our servant, beholden to us for its powers. That principle will later manifest itself in the Constitution in the form of the doctrine of enumerated powers—the idea that government's powers, as enumerated in the document, are delegated to it by the people, who must first have them to delegate. Thus the importance of determining what powers we have, or do not have, to so delegate. Thus also, and again, the logical order of things: rights first, government second, an order found first here, in the Declaration, in the fundamental idea of preexisting rights, rights that preexist government—natural rights, which we have "by nature." Here is more evidence of the Founders' state-of-nature approach to the justificatory undertaking before them.[9]

Notice also that the Founders grounded their moral vision in the language of rights, not that of values, virtues, or other moral notions. Fully and properly fleshed out, the classical theory of rights orders individual acts and social affairs systematically along three deontic modalities: the prohibited, the permitted (the optional), and the required. Objective actions, not subjective mental states, are the primary concern of rights—and, accordingly, of governments. As claims against others denoting adversarial relationships, rights invite moral justification through litigation and, eventually, positive law ordering, as we will see later in this chapter, all for the protection of liberty. In those and similar ways, the theory of rights distinguishes justified from unjustified right claims and thus orders human affairs in ways that values, virtues, and other moral notions are unable to do or do so clearly. In short, rights and correlative obligations are the language of law and liberty. Thus, when they addressed the purpose of government two lines later, the Founders got it right: to secure liberty through law, not to order virtue or impose contested values, much less provide all manner of goods and services. It was live and let live.

"that among these are Life, Liberty, and the Pursuit of Happiness"

The Founders, and later on the Framers of the Constitution and its amendments, could hardly have listed or enumerated all of our rights. On one hand, we have an infinite number of rights, owing to the myriad facts that might enter into their descriptions and the possibilities that language permits. But on the other hand, looked at logically and systematically, we have only one right, the right to be free, from which all other genuine rights, however properly described, may be derived.[10] In a brief, general account of our rights, therefore, one wants to try to capture something of the essence of the matter, which the Founders did when they said that "among" our rights were those to "Life, Liberty, and the Pursuit of Happiness."

To flesh out the Founders' moral vision a bit more, however, we should begin by noticing the implicit distinction in this basic right "to the pursuit of happiness," a distinction between objective rights and subjective values. Clearly, the Founders were not saying that we have a right to happiness but simply to its pursuit. Nor did they tell us how to go about that. They left it to us, provided only that we respect the equal rights of others to pursue their own paths to happiness. Given our different interests and values, we will likely take different paths. As we do, the point simply is that we must respect those differences. We may criticize others' values, of course, and the paths they take, but we may not impose our values on them.[11]

This distinction between objective rights and subjective values, implicit in the right to the pursuit of happiness, is crucial, for it underpins a regime of rights that can be thought of as constituting a basic moral and, eventually, legal framework in which we are all free to plan and live our lives, free from the interference of others. The French *philosophe* Voltaire captured the essence of the matter as it pertains to speech: "I may disagree with what you say, but I will defend to the death your right to say it."[12] You have your values, with which I may disagree, but I will defend your right to live by them, provided only that as you do, you do not violate my or others' rights. In a free society, each of us may make as much or as little of life as we wish and can. As long as we respect the equal rights of others, we are free to choose our paths and are responsible for the choices we make, good and bad alike. That is the essence of freedom. Again, live and let live.

With that basic distinction in mind, we can proceed by drawing on the sources that largely informed the Founders: the English common law, which had evolved over the centuries and had been thought to embody "right reason";[13] and moral philosophers like John Locke, who more than any other can be said to have been the philosophical father of the Declaration, especially through his influence on Thomas Jefferson, its principal author.[14] In deriving more specifically described rights, however, care must be taken to ensure sound derivation and internal consistency; for "rights" dubiously entailed by the first principles of the system or conflicting with one another will undermine the entire rational foundation. Not every good is held by right, after all; we need to separate legitimate from illegitimate right claims.

Consulting the sources just noted, then, we find that theory, experience, and much of custom all show that rights are intimately bound up with the idea of property. Locke put it well: "Lives, Liberties and Estates, which I call by the general Name, *Property*."[15] James Madison, the principal author of the Constitution, made a similar point when he wrote: "As a man is said to have a right to his property, he may be equally said to have a property in his rights."[16] The Founders well understood that all legitimate rights, however described, can be thought of as property and, to aid in casuistry, reduced to property. If what we hold by right can be thought of as property—as something to which we hold a free and clear title or are "entitled"—then we have a place from which to start thinking systematically about our many rights—and thinking about the many claims that may turn out not to be rights. After all, if all legitimate rights can be reduced to property, we will want to know who does and does not have title to that property.[17]

Thus, understanding rights as property—broadly conceived as lives, liberties, and estates—it is but a short step to thinking of right violations as involving the *taking* of that property, the taking of something that *belongs* free and clear—by right—to another. So doing, we can imagine a world in which people are free to live their lives, exercise their liberties, and build and enjoy their estates, provided only that in the process they refrain from taking what is not theirs to take—the lives, liberties, and estates that belong to others.

Notice, then, especially in the context of the modern welfare state, that in a free society there is no obligation to assist others who may need our help, although we are at perfect liberty to offer such assistance. Most, one hopes, will think it good to do so, but we cannot compel that assistance, for that would amount to taking the liberty that belongs to the person so compelled. Association must be voluntary, which is why committing torts, crimes, or contractual breaches—taking others' lives, liberties, or estates—is not only wrong but violates their rights. In a free society, we are free to be virtuous—or not. Indeed, only when virtuous acts are voluntary can they be called virtuous.[18]

Thus, objective rights are not the whole of morality. There is also the vast realm of subjective values that animate and guide our lives. Rights, by contrast, constitute the basic, minimal moral framework within which we are free to flourish, or not, as we wish. As "side-constraints" on our actions, they tell us that we may not take what belongs free and clear to another.[19] We may not commit torts, crimes, or contractual breaches. If we do, new rights and correlative obligations come into being, for we are then obligated to make our victims whole, to restore the prior status quo insofar as possible. Thus, when the Founders spoke of "unalienable" rights, they could have meant only that *others*, including government, may not gratuitously alienate our rights. *We* may alienate them, however, through voluntary contracts; or by committing torts, crimes, or contractual breaches, for which we may be held responsible. In either case, then, whether through voluntary transactions or forced or fraudulent associations, we alienate or extinguish certain rights and obligations and bring new ones into being. Thus does the world of rights and obligations constantly change as we interact over time.[20]

As noted, in the abstract world thus far sketched, we are free to make as much or as little of our lives as we wish and can. In the real world, of course, most will do that mainly not as isolated individuals but through association with others. We come thus to the second basic font of rights: promises or contracts. Entailed by our most basic right to freely act, each of us has a right to associate with others, thereby alienating and creating whatever rights and obligations we wish, provided only that the association be voluntary on all sides, free of fraud regarding what we promise, and respectful of third-party rights. Through such acts—ranging from spot transactions to the creation and conduct of all manner of associations and institutions—people exchange their various holdings, and civil society in all of its rich variety arises.

Similarly, when we commit torts, crimes, or contractual breaches, we also alienate certain rights and obligations and bring new ones into being, but those are more specific. Thus, we create a right in our victims to be made whole and an obligation in ourselves to do so by alienating our right to such of our holdings as may be necessary to satisfy that obligation and right the wrong.

From a base of equal freedom, then, rights and obligations are constantly being alienated and created, either through force or fraud, as just noted, or voluntarily as people arrange and rearrange their affairs with others in ways that they believe will best serve their own interests. The only requirement is that freedom be respected and promises and contracts be kept—failing which, those who take others' freedom, fail to perform as promised, or defraud others must make their victims whole, as detailed in the various branches of the classic common law that treat such matters. As these events unfold, unequal rights and unequal holdings may result, of course. But as long as rights are respected in the process, including by making victims whole, those outcomes will be just, for no one can be heard to complain.

In all of this, however, it is crucial to notice, consistent with state-of-nature theory, that it is private people and institutions that order their affairs, not governments. Notice finally that to this point in the

Declaration, the Founders have addressed only the moral order—the world, when fleshed out, of moral rights and obligations that we have *toward each other.* We now turn to the role of government in securing that order.

"That to secure these Rights, Governments are instituted among Men, deriving their just Powers from the Consent of the Governed"

Were we in a world of perfect information and universal good will, we would need nothing more, for we would all know what rights and obligations we have toward each other and would respect those moral relationships. But universal reason takes us only so far. To complete the account of our rights, we will soon need to introduce values, about which reasonable people can and do have reasonable differences. How much nuisance or risk can we subject our neighbor to, for example, and who is to draw those lines? When contractual terms are unclear or unexpected issues arise, so too may disagreements. And when actual wrongs occur or are alleged, the value-laden procedures for adjudicating them and determining the remedies that may be needed raise only more opportunities for disagreement—and the need for third-party intervention. Finally, all of this is before any enforcement issues arise, so even if we did have perfect knowledge about what rights we have in such cases, we would also have to be of good will, respectfully satisfying our obligations, if not with alacrity, then at least without needing a nudge—or force. Would that we were all that good. Given all of that—and this only scratches the surface—were such disagreements to arise in the state of nature, either alleged injustices would go unaddressed or the parties would resort to force. As Thomas Hobbes famously put it, life in that state would be "solitary, poor, nasty, brutish, and short."[21]

Creating and Empowering a Legitimate Government: Reason and Consent

We arrive, then, at the need for public institutions and procedures to resolve the differences that are inevitable in the state of nature, absent which life there would be intolerable. True, various anarchists have tried to show that we could avoid government and create voluntary institutions to solve the uncertainty and enforcement problems.[22] But that approach has worked, when it has, only for small closely knit groups and only for short periods. And even then, justice has often suffered over time from opportunistic behavior by some or from the group's evolving internal dynamics. In fact, history has been unkind not only to socialist but to anarchist utopians as well. None of which is to say that governments, claiming a monopoly on the use of force, have fared much better—indeed, history speaks volumes on that. Thus, where private arrangements for dispute resolution work well, especially where competition improves such services, they should not be discouraged, much less prohibited. If they can resolve marital difficulties, contractual disagreements, and even tortious wrongs efficiently and peacefully, resort to legal force can be avoided. But such private institutions often work only because a public option stands behind them as a last resort.

Our concern here, however, is not to address the anarchist's every proposal but rather to come to grips with basic questions about moral and political legitimacy. Starting in the state of nature, as the Founders tacitly did, we have outlined a world of moral rights and obligations, at least as far as reason allows; and we have glimpsed the limits of reason and the need for a third party like government to complete that world and secure those rights. But can we create a legitimate government with a monopoly on the use of force, one with legitimate powers designed to address the definitional and enforcement problems, and do it without violating the rights of anyone?

After outlining our basic preexisting natural rights, the Declaration addresses those questions briefly: "That to secure these Rights, Governments are instituted among Men, deriving their just Powers from the Consent of the Governed." Thus, reason and consent underpin political and legal legitimacy. Reason first justifies our preexisting natural rights. Consent then justifies government and its powers, including those needed to flesh out and enforce our rights. How could it be otherwise? We cannot rightly force people out of the state of nature; nor can we take from them powers they rightly have. In the state of nature we all have Locke's "Executive Power," the right to define our rights more precisely and then secure them.[23] Can we create a government and grant it those powers, to be exercised on our behalf, without violating preexisting rights in the process? We'll first address the creation issue,[24] then consider government's powers, and finally ask if government can have purposes beyond securing our rights. That will take us to a question that deeply divides Americans today: What is the proper role of government?

Because those issues are complex and subtle, we can address them here only at a fairly general level. To do that, however, we will take the same course we took earlier in the chapter, the course that Locke took when he, too, thought about such questions; but we will press the issues a bit further than Locke did and ask first what rights we would have toward securing our various rights if there were no government, if we were in the state of nature. Those are the rights that come into play only after the rights outlined previously have been, or are about to be, violated. Merely stating the matter, however, reveals its complexity. For we are dealing now with a realm of considerable uncertainty in which, again, principles of reason go only so far. To be sure, enforcement rights must be justified with reference to the rights we have to be secured. But in addition, and beyond the question of derivation, these enforcement rights must be exercised in ways that respect the rights to be secured. Indeed, we can hardly violate rights in the name of securing rights and be thought to be doing so by right.[25]

Creating Government: The Problem of Consent

If our move from the state of nature to a world with a government empowered to secure our rights requires our consent to be legitimate, as the Declaration says, two problems immediately arise. First, practically, is the absence in the state of nature of any public institutions through which to execute this political consent. And second, more important theoretically, if this move is to respect the equal rights of all equally, we will need *unanimous* consent.[26] Yet rarely if ever do we get unanimity with such matters. Indeed, if the need for government arises because reason has run its course, and we now disagree over how to complete the account of our rights, why should we expect agreement over the far more complex and fraught institutional arrangements for resolving those disputes—government?

We see, then, that just as the reach of reason in discerning our rights is limited, so too, *a fortiori*, is consent limited here, for the universal right to freedom that we derived earlier appears to preclude us from forcing others into our public world under governmental rule. Given our basic right to freedom, only those who consent may rightly be bound by government. But it is more complicated still, because consent reaches well beyond the primordial individual consent that we imagine taking place in some theoretical "original position." Perhaps America came closer to satisfying that ideal "origination" of government than any other nation, but even in America the franchise was limited. Most who would be bound by the Constitution did not vote; the voting was mostly not direct but rather for delegates to state ratifying conventions; and many delegates voted against the proposed Constitution. Moreover, once that document was ratified, making it positive law, and government was instituted, most voting since has not been directly for powers or policies but for candidates for the offices set forth therein—and again, there were electoral losers in all of this, bound nonetheless by the laws they had voted indirectly against.

Classical liberals understood this problem, of course, which is why they crafted more complex consent-based rationales for political legitimacy. But their arguments come up short. Again, the basic question here is whether consent short of unanimity can render a government or its powers thus created morally legitimate. Majoritarianism will not avail, of course, for on any given issue, starting with the creation of government itself, it amounts to the majority compelling the minority to its will when the minority, by definition, has not consented. So too, the "social contract" fails; by positing that we all agree *originally* to be bound thereafter by the majority or by some other fraction of the whole, it simply assumes unanimity in the original position while also failing to solve the problem posed by later generations who were never in that position and hence did not consent. Finally, the "tacit consent" argument—if you stay, you have implicitly agreed to be bound—fails also. Aiming to overcome the generational problem, the majority puts the minority to a choice between two of its entitlements: its right to stay, and its right not to be ruled by the majority. Given our basic right to be free, the majority must justify its claim to rule, failing which it rules by force, not by right, thus arguing in a circle by assuming that right.

Clearly, there are real problems with resting political legitimacy on the consent of the governed, starting with this most fundamental of questions concerning the creation of a government. When we turn to the powers of government and their execution, as we soon will, the problems with consent-based justifications only grow. When the electoral process is complicated by representation, political parties, voting by legislative districts, gerrymandering, ranked-choice voting, and other such electoral procedures, variations of which we see in all democracies; and when all we are left with is a single vote, binding all for a period of time, it simply strains credulity to say that such processes, reflecting the consent of some to some things, render the outcome legitimate. Whatever the record of democracies toward disciplining government—plainly, it is mixed—if we are serious about moral and political legitimacy, we need to acknowledge the limits of political consent.

The attraction of democracy is that "we the people" control our government: Just as we controlled our individual lives in the state of nature, the argument goes, so too do we control our collective lives once we create a democracy. But that's a myth. The individual control we each have in the state of nature is drastically diminished when collectivized. We trade the complete control we each had over our own lives for a periodic vote over vast issues affecting us in countless ways, leaving us with little control—save to leave the collective, if allowed. During the 1960s, when the slogan "power to the people" was in vogue, University of Chicago economist Milton Friedman famously remarked that he agreed—save for the definite article.

To be sure, as Winston Churchill famously implied, other things being equal, it is better to have at least some control over one's government than none, as in nondemocratic regimes.[27] But if we're serious about maximizing our freedom, it is far better to delegate as little control to the collective as necessary and to reserve as much *individual* control as possible. (In truth, it is best to *optimize* our freedom, about which more below.) Of course, there will always be those who are uncomfortable with or even frightened by having the right and responsibility of making decisions over their own lives, but what right have they to take that right from the rest of us? And there will always be those who encourage delegating power to government, confident that they will be in positions to wield it.

The Basic Political Presumption: Government as a "Necessary Evil"

What, then, are we to say? Again, the dilemma is this: We leave the state of nature to create a government that will enable us to avoid arbitrary force to resolve differences that must be resolved, but government itself is a forced association, as anyone who has ever been in the minority on some important public question knows. Are we to conclude, then, that the anarchist is right, that government *as such* is illegitimate? Strictly speaking, we are, even if we cannot live with that answer, practically. We will revisit and qualify that disquieting conclusion shortly. But for now, notice the silver lining in this dilemma: the limited government implications.

We see, then, that for practical reasons, the Declaration's consent requirement for political legitimacy cannot really be satisfied, for in reality it leads not to universal consent but, at best, to democratic procedures like supermajoritarian constitutional ratification and periodic majoritarian voting, the latter, most often, not to approve particular powers or policies but to fill offices with officials who may or may not exercise those powers or pursue those policies. Democratic procedures bring us closer to moral and political legitimacy than we'd be without them. But as history shows, they still leave us with the prospect of both majoritarian and, more often, special interest tyranny, which the Founders and Framers, keen students of history, well understood and tried to guard against, as we will see. Thus, if moral and political legitimacy are our ultimate concerns, the anarchist cannot be ignored—except on practical grounds. Given the boundless inconveniences of life in the state of nature, only a fanatic would stay there. Yet fanatics too have rights.

Thus, as we force such recalcitrants out of the state of nature and into our emerging political world, or force them to leave the polity, we ourselves, being both rational and practical, are forced to face the implications of this brief, systematic analysis of political consent. Yet those implications, *mirabile dictu*, turn out to be salutary. In fact, they give us a crucial and far-reaching framework for going forward. Because reason justifies our right to freedom and consent justifies association, including the association that purports to govern and, in fact, will be a government; because absent such actual consent, that institution will amount to a forced association for those who haven't consented; because life in the state of nature is unbearable, practically, "forcing" us to leave it, as it were; and because life under government entails both a forced association in itself and many other forced associations as government unfolds and expands, we arrive at a clear and inescapable moral presumption *against* doing things through government, where force is inevitable, and a clear and inescapable presumption *for* individual liberty, with a heavy burden on those who want to do things through government to show why they must be done there rather than left to the private sector where they can be done freely and hence in violation of the rights of no one. Government, in short, should be a *last* resort, turned to only when freedom fails to protect our rights. Hold that thought. It is rich with implications.

There, in a nutshell, is the moral and political argument for *limited* government, which Thomas Paine stated succinctly: "Government, even in its best state, is but a necessary evil; in its worst state, an intolerable one."[28] Necessary, for the reasons we have canvassed, but evil because government compels our involvement in matters many of us may want no part of—and it gets worse as government grows. On the question of moral and political legitimacy, therefore, the Founders got it right. Modern progressives who turn so regularly to government not as a last but as a first or early resort, as do modern conservatives oftentimes, get it wrong, not simply practically but morally, seemingly oblivious to the essential character of government as a forced association, threatening and often using force in all it does—even when its ends and means are otherwise perfectly legitimate and, indeed, must be pursued, not just for legal but for moral reasons too.

Quite apart, then, from how actual governments have been brought into being, if the consent of the governed matters for the legitimacy of a government's very existence, and actual consent from only a part of the governed is the best we can do as a practical matter, then government truly *is* different, morally, from private associations. It claims and mostly has a monopoly on the use of force. And we do not "join" government like we join private associations. At bottom it is a forced association with an air of illegitimacy about it. Not for nothing did the Founders and Framers keep government at arm's length.

But given the practical necessity of government, prudence suggests that we search for arguments that might lend this institution a bit more legitimacy—while still preserving the basic presumption. Here, we will do that by drawing from a consideration of risk. Again, we are faced with the lack of consent from the few holdouts who want to remain in the state of nature. Like us, they too claim the right to interpret and enforce their rights—their right of self-defense—as an implication of their right to be free. But unlike them, we have a keener sense of the risk that *individual* self-enforcement entails for all of us and a greater appreciation of the need, accordingly, to reduce that risk—as an exercise, indeed, of *our* rights of self-defense. We're more risk-averse than they appear to be—or, at least, we view enforcement by individuals as riskier than by government, about which there are reasonable differences, not surprisingly. It is the risk that individual self-defense poses that, for us, justifies institutionalizing and regularizing our enforcement rights to reduce the risk—not entirely, but enough to justify, at least for us, the creation of government for that purpose. Thus, our right of self-defense justifies for us, in turn, the limited force required to bring government over all into being. In a context where there are no bright lines, risk, yet where we cannot just walk away if rights are to be enforced efficiently and safely, we are simply defending ourselves, by right.

To be clear, that is not an apodictic argument, for assessments of risk, however well-reasoned, are rarely dispositive. Rather, we turn to it because we are at an impasse arising from risk in an especially acute, basic context requiring resolution: enforcement. If we disagree about our enforcement rights in the state of nature—not about the broad principles but about their more precise contours and applications—we cannot simply agree to disagree and walk away, for our rights will then be little more than aspirational—or private force will result (apart from that which, admittedly, we employ here to bring government about). To avoid either outcome—and to protect the rights at issue—we will need binding public institutions. That necessity will itself lend a measure of legitimacy to the government we create for that purpose.

True, the argument does not address the particular character and scope of the enforcement rights that are entailed by our right of self-defense, which could change as our assessment of risk changes. But it is implicit in the Declaration's consent requirement. When we are thus "forced" to consent, at least as best can be done in this uncertain context of risk, we grant government enforcement powers we already have as individuals in the state of nature. To that extent, therefore, they are legitimate.

Soon we will see two related arguments that will lend a bit more legitimacy both to government and to its powers, but the argument just outlined is enough to get us out of the state of nature and into a world with a government. Creating a government from scratch in a state of nature entails many other practical, institutional, and administrative considerations, of course. Who counts as a member of the polity? What geographical boundaries define our jurisdiction? What institutional arrangements will best serve the government's functions? How to select officials? Those and other such practical questions remain to be addressed. Important as they are, however, our central concern going forward will be less with such matters than with the legitimacy of governmental powers that bear directly on individuals.

At a broader level, of course, we can speak of governments as being more or less legitimate, and that is no small matter. Thus, a government that arises through a majority or, better still, a supermajority vote of the governed will be seen as more legitimate, other things equal, than one that is forced on the governed by a cabal, to say nothing of one that is imposed by outside powers. And it will be thought so because, as the Declaration implies, consent counts toward legitimacy—and the more the better. But here we have to be careful: We have to distinguish between a *government's* legitimacy—for purposes of international diplomacy, for example—and the legitimacy of its *powers and actions*. Thus the other-things-being-equal caveat just mentioned. Once we move beyond original consent, however, tacit consent thereafter—people not leaving, if they can—will count too, but it will not be the only or even the most important measure of a government's legitimacy. We could have supermajoritarian tyranny, for example. A more important measure, therefore, will be whether a government, even if imposed on a people, respects rights. That will bear in turn on the perceived and actual legitimacy of the regime itself. To that issue we now turn.

Empowering Government: Basic Powers and Their Execution

With the presumption against resorting to government still securely before us, we now have a government in place with at least a modicum of legitimacy based simply on how it arose, much like our own federal and state governments. But in this still theoretical world we have yet to determine the legitimacy of this government's powers and the execution of those powers as they concern individuals. Here again, consent counts, the Declaration says, but not only consent. In fact, just as consent goes only so far in lending legitimacy to the *creation* of a government, so too it does *a fortiori* in lending legitimacy to government's *powers* and the *execution* of those powers. A power that allowed government arbitrarily to take from *A* to give to *B*, for example, would be illegitimate, even if a supermajority consented to it: first, because *A* has a preexisting right to what is his (no line-drawing problem here, as with risk); and second, because no one had such a power to yield up to government in the first place. Thus, once we get past the creation of a government and ask whether its powers and the execution of those powers are legitimate, individual rights loom large, including the rights we do *not* have and thus cannot rightly give to government to be exercised by it as powers.[29]

The police power

We can address those issues in a general way by distinguishing three basic powers that we might grant to government, ranging from the most to the least legitimate. The first has come to be called the general police power, which in America belongs to the states, the federal government having only a limited police power.[30] The most basic of government's powers, the police power is held by all in the state of nature, where we have the power to define our rights more fully and then secure them—Locke's "Executive Power." Consistent with our discussion of risk earlier in this chapter, when we authorize a government through a constitution, we grant it various powers in the process, including the police power, as the Declaration says. That power authorizes the government thus created to recognize our natural and moral rights, to define them more than reason alone allows, and to secure them against domestic and foreign threats, ex ante and ex post. By tradition, the police power has also been used by government to regulate "health, safety, and morals" and to provide for the "common good" or "general welfare."

Because each of us had the state-of-nature version of the police power, it cannot be said that we gave government a power that was not ours to give. Thus, our having granted government that power takes nothing from its legitimacy. The only person who could be heard to complain is the anarchist who made no such delegation but is now mostly prevented from exercising his enforcement power by virtue of the government having a monopoly on the use of force.[31] Fortunately, such anarchists are few. Once government has the police power, it must be exercised in a right-respecting way, of course. Due process rights loom large here. But so too must the scope of the power be restrained.

Much of the health and safety regulation government does today pursuant to its police power, including a good measure of its environmental regulation, is simply part of its power to define our rights more precisely and then secure them. Those powers can be misused, of course, as when government fails adequately to take costs and benefits and their distribution into account when defining the relevant rights and obligations, or when it wrongly assigns responsibility. But the power itself, properly used, is legitimate. Indeed, it is precisely because we do not agree in the state of nature about where to draw many such lines or who may be liable that we turn to a third party to adjudicate those differences.

But the regulation of "morals" through the police power is harder to justify in the name of protecting rights. In colonial days, for example, sumptuary laws regulated extravagant apparel. In our own time, states have used their police power to criminalize interracial marriage, the sale and use of contraceptives, various sexual practices and lifestyles, and more. Here we have the regulation of behavior and activities that merely offend enough people to generate a demand for the regulation—majoritarian tyranny concerning behavior that usually violates no one's rights. True, some cases may implicate rights, especially the rights of children. But in other cases the police power is used to regulate or ban otherwise rightful behavior or activities, however offensive, everything from blasphemy to hate speech, alcohol consumption, smoking, drug use, prostitution, pornography, gambling, public nudity, bull and cock fighting, wanton cruelty to animals, and more. Just to be clear, I would be among the first to support prohibiting some of that, like public nudity or wanton cruelty to animals, though not in the name of protecting rights—it is difficult enough to show that *humans* have rights, much less animals—but in the name of a vague idea like "decency" or a "humane society." The problem, of course, is that once you do that, you are on a slippery slope, at the bottom of which is tyranny—to say nothing of the corruption that has ever attended the zealous prohibition of vice. In this domain, a strong but rebuttable presumption against government looms large, as discussed earlier, almost as large as good judgment.

Perhaps some of that morals regulation can be justified as serving the "common good," but the police power is more easily justified when it is employed to provide what economists call "public goods," goods enjoyed roughly equally by all but not likely to be provided privately in a state of nature due to the "free-rider" problem.[32] Genuine public goods like law enforcement, national defense, clean air and water, and certain infrastructure are characterized by "nonexcludability" and "nonrivalrous consumption," meaning that once they are provided by some, others cannot be excluded from enjoying them (nonexcludability), and the marginal cost of another person's consuming them, once they have been produced, is zero (nonrivalrous consumption). In the state of nature, even if we could overcome the coordination problems, private parties would be disinclined to provide such goods if there are substantial numbers of free riders—people willing to enjoy but unwilling to bear their share of the costs of such goods—so they generally will not be produced. It is crucial, however, to distinguish these goods from private goods like education, housing, health care, childcare, retirement security, and so on, which may be goods for all but which individuals can and will provide for themselves through markets to whatever extent they wish and can. In fact, a useful test for whether a good is public or private is whether the market is already providing it; education and housing, for example, are likely goods for all, but they are readily available in the private market.

Thus, here, with due respect for government's duty to treat all equally, we have a proper function of government that goes beyond the strict protection of rights. And in addition to our earlier argument lending legitimacy to government from a concern about the risks of private enforcement in the state of nature, we now have another rationale for government, one that eases the air of illegitimacy that arises from the absence of actual consent. For government—created ultimately through force, to be sure—will enable the production of goods that would otherwise not be produced, yielding roughly equal implicit compensation and a net gain for all. Put it this way: Better that we all, as individuals, police our own rights, our air quality, our health during pandemics, and threats from abroad, or forgo basic infrastructure? Quite apart from the absence of genuine public goods in the state of nature, the positive gains for all from the public provision of such goods will render untenable any arguments against government based on the absence of actual unanimous consent. It is the opposite with the public provision of private goods, where costs and benefits are invariably distributed unequally, yielding a gain for some and a loss for others. For that reason, it is crucial to distinguish genuine public goods from goods that are private and thus will be provided individually as the beneficiaries may wish and can, weighing their own costs and benefits.[33] We will return to this point after we discuss a second basic power of government, eminent domain.

Eminent domain

In general, then, the police power, properly executed and constrained to little more than its core functions of securing our rights and providing genuine public goods, is the most legitimate of the powers we might grant to government, for we all had that power in the state of nature, save for the morals and public goods parts. Not so with government's second great power, eminent domain, an instrumental power that enables government to take private property for public use while executing another power or pursuing another end like building a military base or a public road, but only if just compensation is paid to the owner from whom the property is taken. In the state of nature, none of us had a right to take our neighbor's property without his consent, even if we did put it to a better or public use and paid him just compensation. Known in the 17th and 18th centuries as the "despotic power," eminent domain is said often to be an "inherent" power of government. From a consideration of first principles, however, to say nothing of circularity, there are no inherent powers of government, only powers delegated by the people as enumerated in a constitution. How, then, can eminent domain be said to be legitimate if none of us had such a power in the state of nature and thus had it to delegate?

In America, insofar as our limited consent can be said to justify a power, there is, first, the language of the Constitution's Fifth Amendment, "nor shall private property be taken for public use without just compensation," which implicitly recognizes the power of eminent domain while explicitly recognizing the right of just compensation pursuant to its use. But second, economists justify eminent domain as "Pareto superior," which means that at least one party is made better off by its use—here, the public, as evidenced by its willingness to pay—and no one is made worse off because the owner gets just compensation, meaning that the owner is indifferent as to whether he keeps the property or gets the compensation. Thus, when so used, because the property is worth more to the public than the cost of obtaining it, while the owner remains indifferent, eminent domain increases net social welfare by moving property to a higher valued use: one winner, us, and no losers.

Unfortunately, rarely in practice does the owner get just compensation. At best, the owner ordinarily gets market value, which is not just compensation if his property is not up for sale, for that means that it is worth more to the owner than the amount it would fetch if on the market. Because it is a despotic power, eminent domain should be used only when necessary, as when a holdout takes advantage of his "monopoly" situation to demand exorbitant compensation for the last parcel needed to complete a public road. Otherwise, just like with any private party, government should bargain for the property it needs, not use its power to get property "on the cheap." For the same reason, "public use" should be read narrowly, not as "public benefit," which is an open sesame for the promiscuous use of the power. Finally, when government provides the public with goods like lovely views or wildlife habitat by restricting a property owner's otherwise legitimate uses, thus devaluing the property, eminent domain should apply to compensate the owner for his losses, just like when the entire property is taken.

Notice, then, that the Pareto superior rationale for eminent domain is not unlike both the earlier risk-based rationale for creating government and the constructive consent rationale for public goods. And similar rationales come to the fore in many other cases, like oil and gas extraction, for in each such case, faced with impediments to a fully voluntary agreement—coordination problems, high transaction costs, free riders, and holdouts, for which the "pure" libertarian theory based on actual consent has no answer—an implicit equal compensation or efficiency argument can be employed, showing no actual loss for anyone (including the anarchist) and a net gain for all. Still, to be morally legitimate, to overcome any absence of actual consent, the compensation must be roughly equal for all and sufficient to warrant the bargain. When invoking such an approach, we must be careful, of course, for it can easily be extended to situations where individual choice and responsibility should remain or where we are not *all* better off. But when we all are better off, what rational person would not consent to such an outcome? Here, in short, we have arguments based on constructive consent that reasonably satisfy the Declaration's consent requirement.

The redistributive power

If the eminent domain power is less legitimate than the police power, prima facie, the third great power of government, the nonegalitarian redistributive power, is altogether illegitimate, yet today it describes government's main business—transferring property, including liberty, from *A* to *B*. This power takes two forms: material and regulatory. Material redistribution is done through government's power to tax and spend. Regulatory redistribution is done by prohibiting some from doing what they would otherwise have a right to do or requiring them to do what they would otherwise have a right not to do, all for the benefit of others. As such, regulatory redistribution is distinct from the legitimate regulation that is needed to flesh out and enforce our rights, which is entailed by the police power. And unlike with eminent domain or the constructive consent cases, here there are no roughly equal benefits for all. Rather, we get winners and losers.

Taxation is not illegitimate per se. Along lines discussed earlier, it is part of the bargain we strike in the original position: We no longer have to police our own rights; we pay government to do it for us because we believe that on balance it is safer and more efficient than trying to do it ourselves; so we tax ourselves to pay for the service, absent which there would be no taxes—or service. Altogether different is redistributive taxation, designed expressly to transfer funds from *A* to *B*, to take from *A* and give to *B*. Yet even legitimate taxation raises problems; for government, belonging to all of us, must treat us all equally, a notoriously difficult principle to apply, even where there are objective, quantifiable measures, as with taxation. A word or two on this morally fraught subject will suffice.

A use tax might be a good place to start because it seems to satisfy the equal treatment principle by tying the beneficiary of the public service to the cost of providing it, at least in principle. Taxation for law enforcement might be thought of as a kind of use tax. But to respect our right to equal treatment by government, a use tax needs to be carefully constructed and applied. Gasoline taxes, for example, are meant to impose the costs of public roads proportionally on those who use them, but people with electric vehicles often escape the tax, and the funds collected are often redirected to public transportation, so what starts out as a use tax can easily become redistributive taxation.

An equal head tax would satisfy equal treatment, but of course its effects would be unequal due to the unequal distribution of individual wealth; and the benefits received would be unequal due to unequal individual circumstances. Should equality be a function of the tax itself—$10 a head—or should we take its effect into account such that a $10 tax on a person with assets of $100 and a $100 tax on a person with assets of $1,000 satisfies equal treatment? Then too, should equal treatment take causal and beneficial factors into account? Should criminals who cause greater need for law enforcement pay more in taxes, for example, or should those who need more protection because they have more to lose from crime pay more? A flat income tax tends toward equality of effect but not equality per se because high earners pay more. A graduated income tax satisfies neither; it simply takes advantage of the diminishing marginal value of increasing income and wealth. Finally, a consumption tax, by affording more tax choices to the taxpayer, might seem to satisfy equal treatment, but its regressive effects suggest otherwise.

The conclusion to be drawn from this brief, inconclusive discussion—which hasn't even mentioned the many other forms of taxation, much less the use of taxation for extraneous policy objectives—is straightforward: Since it is nigh on impossible to construct a tax system that treats all equally, we can ameliorate that problem only by demanding fewer goods and services from government. Markets, including insurance markets where companies are allowed to discriminate according to actuarial risks, match buyers and sellers far more equitably and efficiently than monopoly government ever could. Here too, then, the moral principle of equal treatment by government should impel us to do as little as necessary through government and as much as possible in the private sector.

Yet the course of the past century has been mostly in the other direction: ever more governmental goods and taxation not even pretending to be for such things but instead for straightforward redistribution. When we include countless forms of regulatory redistribution—more difficult to quantify but doubtless more extensive today than material redistribution because it is done "off-budget" and hence less noticeably than taxation—we have a massive transfer society. And the transfers are not executed efficiently through individual choices in free markets but inefficiently by government planners, confident that they can order our affairs better than we ourselves can, left to our own devices.[34]

To be clear, I do not mean to be understood as arguing that once we leave the state of nature and establish government, we are morally prohibited from helping the unfortunate of various kinds through public transfer programs. Rather, I am arguing, as a matter of principle, that we not do so in the name of "rights" or as "entitlements" rather than, under the circumstances, from necessity, as a last resort, with the burden of persuasion on those who would replace private with public action; for treating public charity as a matter of right strips us of the moral discipline the theory of rights affords.[35] Americans have always been a generous people. We still are. For much of our history we did not rely for the most part on public charity. With the rise of Progressivism, however, the push was on not simply to supplement but to "crowd out" private charity, replacing it with public charity undertaken by "professional" social workers. Alas, *forcing* people to "do good" through government undermines the moral order by undermining the individual responsibility that underpins freedom. As earlier noted, there is no virtue in forced beneficence.[36]

But the modern welfare state is only partly about helping the unfortunate. Today, it reaches far beyond with countless middle-class, upper-class, and corporate welfare schemes, privileges, and immunities that introduce perverse incentives not only against ending but also for expanding and multiplying those programs. Indeed, many such schemes are not even seen as "welfare." To the extent that government controls or at least influences the nation's monetary system, for example, it can move interest rates to below the rate of inflation, thus favoring both government borrowing and that of favored private entities while transferring wealth from savers and creditors to debtors, including the government itself. Taken together, all of this, of course, is leading us increasingly toward insolvency while undermining our character. As history demonstrates—in fact, is demonstrating today with our uncontrolled, unsustainable public debt—this cannot end well.[37]

What are we to say, though, when it appears, as in modern democracies, including our own, that large majorities sometimes willingly support an ever-expanding state? Given that a minority does not, we have here the classic problem of the tyranny of the majority, pitting individual rights against majoritarian consent, the individual against the collective—at bottom, the problem of political consent as a ground for legitimacy, seeming to justify that tyranny. And this is not limited to typical economic redistributive schemes involving retirement, health care, education, labor unionization, and the like. Grounded in their histories, many nations today, even democratic nations, still self-identify, redistribute, or regulate to some extent along religious, racial, ethnic, or other discriminatory lines. Are we to say that all of this is morally illegitimate? Insofar as equal treatment is concerned, we are, although there may be some exceptions for clear historical or security reasons, such as with the state of Israel.

When majoritarian democracy is privileged over individual liberty other than for basic functions like line-drawing to flesh out our natural and moral rights or providing genuine public goods—that is, when democracy is the presumption and liberty becomes its contingent product—we have three basic models: one fully coercive, one less so, one not so. The first illegitimate model compels all citizens to participate in the public program, sometimes restricting even religious freedom—seen now in certain health care and antidiscrimination contexts. The less illegitimate model makes participation in such programs voluntary, thus allowing for minority rights. Rarely, of course, is that model entirely voluntary. Instead, one might be allowed to opt out in favor of a private service, yet still be taxed for the public program, as with public education. Best would be the third model, which would allow individuals to opt out entirely from the program, including from any tax or regulation pertaining to it, the better to be able to afford (or to forgo) a private service.

In America today, we are well along a socialization continuum running from limited to largely unlimited government—and many are urging us to go even farther. No wonder we are so divided. That raises a basic question: Who asked for all of these programs and the accompanying taxation, regulation, and public debt? The short answer is that too many of us have—believing, to be sure, the "free stuff" promises of the politicians we have elected. Thus, many have lost touch with the vision set forth in our Founding document, while many more have never been exposed, given how civics is too often taught today, to the idea that government exists not to solve our every problem but to enable us, through the rule of law, to face the challenges of life by living lives of freedom and dignity. Democracy is not an end in itself. Nor is it a legitimate means, certainly, for compelling others to join in public projects they may want no part of. In fact, at bottom, America is not really a democracy in the classic sense of that idea. It is a constitutional republic, dedicated to securing for each of us the blessings of liberty: "That to secure these *Rights*, Governments are instituted among Men, deriving their *just* Powers from the Consent of the Governed."

Notes

1. I have discussed the issue of legitimacy more fully in Roger Pilon, "Individual Rights, Democracy, and Constitutional Order: On the Foundations of Legitimacy," *Cato Journal* 11, no. 3 (1992): 373–90.

2. In the state-of-nature tradition, the Founders drew primarily from John Locke's "Second Treatise of Government" (1690), in *Two Treatises of Government*, ed. Peter Laslett (Mentor, 1965). For a more recent argument in that tradition, see Robert Nozick, *Anarchy, State, and Utopia* (Basic Books, 1974).

3. On the tradition of moral rationality, see Alan Gewirth, *Reason and Morality* (University of Chicago Press, 1978); and Roger Pilon, "A Theory of Rights: Toward Limited Government" (PhD diss., University of Chicago, 1979).

4. For useful discussions of the ideological currents surrounding the Declaration, see Bernard Bailyn, *The Ideological Origins of the American Revolution* (Belknap, 1967); Carl L. Becker, *The Declaration of Independence: A Study in the History of Political Ideas* (Harcourt, Brace and Company, 1922; repr., Vintage, 1958); and Morton White, *The Philosophy of the American Revolution* (Oxford University Press, 1978).

5. See Richard A. Epstein, *Simple Rules for a Complex World* (Harvard University Press, 1995).

6. See Maurice Cranston, "Human Rights, Real and Supposed," in *Political Theory and the Rights of Man*, ed. D.D. Raphael (Indiana University Press, 1967), pp. 43–53; Roger Pilon, "Ordering Rights Consistently: Or What We Do and Do Not Have Rights To," *Georgia Law Review* 13, no. 4 (1979): 1171–96.

7. See Wesley Newcomb Hohfeld, *Fundamental Legal Conceptions as Applied in Judicial Reasoning* (Yale University Press, 1946).

8. See also Roger Pilon, "On Moral and Legal Justification," *Southwestern University Law Review* 11, no. 4 (1979): 1327–44.

9. I have discussed the constitutional aspects of this point more fully in Roger Pilon, "A Government of Limited Powers," in *Cato Handbook for Congress* (Cato Institute, 1995), pp. 17–34; reprinted as "Restoring Constitutional Government," in *Cato's Letter*, no. 9, Cato Institute, 1995.

10. See H. L. A. Hart, "Are There Any Natural Rights?," *Philosophical Review* 64 (1955): 175–91.

11. None of this is to say, of course, that no values are "better" than others or that we cannot reason about values. Clearly, we do reason about values; and we can make powerful prudential arguments about which values are superior to others. But in the end, values are subjective in the sense that, unlike natural rights, they vary from person to person; and in the more analytical sense that statements about values are neither true nor false, there being no ultimate criterion of value that is immune to skeptical challenge. I have discussed this issue more fully in Roger Pilon, "The Right to Do Wrong," in *Flag-Burning, Discrimination, and the Right to Do Wrong*, ed. Roger Pilon (Cato Institute, 1990), pp. 1–7; repr. in *The Libertarian Reader*, ed. David Boaz (The Free Press, 1997), pp. 197–201; and Roger Pilon, untitled essay in "E Pluribus Unum? A Symposium on Pluralism and Public Policy," The American Jewish Committee, Washington, DC, 1997, pp. 61–64.

12. Evelyn Beatrice Hall, *The Friends of Voltaire* (G. P. Putnam's Sons, 1907), p. 199. This line may be Hall's paraphrase of Voltaire's views rather than a direct quotation.

13. Edward S. Corwin, *The "Higher Law" Background of American Constitutional Law* (Cornell University Press, 1995), p. 26.

14. See especially Locke, "Second Treatise of Government."

15. Locke, "Second Treatise of Government," para. 123 (emphasis in original).

16. James Madison, "Property," *National Gazette* 1, no. 44 (March 29, 1792): 174–75; repr. in *Letters and Other Writings of James Madison*, vol. 4, *1829–1836* (Philadelphia, 1865), pp. 478–80.

17. I have developed these points more fully in Pilon, "Ordering Rights Consistently."

18. I have discussed this issue more fully in Pilon, "Ordering Rights Consistently." See also James M. Ratcliffe, ed., *The Good Samaritan and the Law* (Doubleday, 1966).

19. See Nozick, *Anarchy, State, and Utopia*.

20. Sometimes we use the word "forfeit" to mean "alienate" by one's own actions; for example, a murderer is said to have forfeited or alienated his right to his liberty and perhaps to his life. Likewise, through promise or contract, we alienate and create rights and obligations on a regular basis, as will be discussed shortly. Often, however, the question whether we can alienate various of our rights is conflated with the question whether a given right, having been alienated to another person, will be secured or enforced. Care must be taken to notice that those are separate questions. In particular, in the nature of things—given the vagaries of life—not every right, including rights we may have alienated to others, can or should be enforced.

21. Thomas Hobbes, *Leviathan*, ed. J. C. A. Gaskin (Oxford University Press, 2008), p. 76.

22. See, for example, Bruce Benson, *The Enterprise of Law: Justice Without the State* (Pacific Research Institute for Public Policy, 1990). For a discussion of how that might work, but would ultimately fail, see Nozick, *Anarchy, State, and Utopia*, part III.

23. Locke, "Second Treatise of Government," para. 13.

24. Although the Declaration speaks of just or legitimate powers, not just or legitimate governments, the legitimacy of government itself, as an institution, is a function, presumably, of our having "instituted" it and hence, to that extent, consented to come under its rule. Just how much that consent serves to lend legitimacy to ongoing governments is a question we take up next, by implication, when we consider whether consent justifies powers more extensive than the enforcement power and, more generally, whether consent justifies anything in the political context.

25. It is no accident that the Fourth Amendment speaks of the right to be free from "unreasonable" searches and seizures; that it requires "probable" cause before warrants can be issued; and that the Eighth Amendment speaks of "excessive" bail and of "cruel and unusual" punishment. Those areas of the law, in their nature, require value judgments. It would have been highly imprudent for Madison, when drafting the Bill of Rights during the first Congress, to have drawn those provisions more precisely.

26. It is noteworthy that the Constitution's ratification clause, Article VII, reflects the social contract model of legitimacy, thus consent: "The Ratification of the Conventions of nine States, shall be sufficient for the Establishment of this

Constitution *between the States so ratifying the Same*" (emphasis added). Setting aside the problem posed by the consent coming from state conventions rather than from the people directly, the point to notice is that only those states that had ratified the Constitution could be bound by it. Thus, it took *unanimity*, among at least nine states, to get the Constitution off the ground; and, as a corollary, that consent bound only those states.

27. Winston Churchill, speech given in the House of Commons, November 11, 1947, London, England.

28. Thomas Paine, *Common Sense* (Philadelphia, 1776).

29. However, just as individuals can contract around otherwise wrongful actions—for example, boxers before they enter the ring—so too, through "constructive consent," we *could* grant government powers that none of us had in the state of nature. Hold that thought; we will develop it shortly.

30. Consistent with federalism principles, such police power as the federal government has applies only over federal territory, wrongs against federal officials, or the enforcement of federal law, which is why most criminal and civil enforcement in America is undertaken by state agencies.

31. At this point in our argument, the justification for government's monopoly on the use of force, except when self-help is necessary, rests on the need to avoid the risks of individual enforcement in the state of nature, as discussed earlier.

32. The classic work on public goods was by James M. Buchanan, *The Demand and Supply of Public Goods* (Rand McNally & Co., 1968).

33. Here is Abraham Lincoln on this point: "Government is a combination of the people of a country to effect certain objects by joint effort. . . . The legitimate object of government is to do for a community of people whatever they need to have done, but cannot do at all, or cannot so well do, for themselves, in their separate and individual capacities." Abraham Lincoln, "The Nature and Objects of Government, with Special Reference to Slavery," in *Life and Works of Abraham Lincoln*, ed. Marion Mills Miller, vol. 3 (The Current Literature Publishing Company, 1907).

34. Perhaps no one advocated this course toward more government planning more frankly than Columbia University's Rexford Tugwell, a member of Franklin Roosevelt's "Brain Trust" and a principal architect of the seminal New Deal programs that have grown and grown more numerous ever since. Writing early in 1932 in the *American Economic Review*, Tugwell said: "fundamental changes of attitude, new disciplines, revised legal structures, *unaccustomed limitations on activity*, are all necessary if we are to plan. This amounts, in fact, to the abandonment, finally, of *laissez faire*. It amounts, practically, *to the abolition of 'business.' This is what planning calls for.*" We aren't quite there yet, but give it time (emphasis added). Rexford Tugwell, "The Principle of Planning and the Institution of Laissez Faire," *American Economic Review* 22, no. 1 (March, 1932): 75–92, p. 76.

35. A core conceptual problem with the United Nations' 1948 Universal Declaration of Human Rights, promoted assiduously by Eleanor Roosevelt, is its inclusion of "social, economic, and cultural rights" (mostly redistributive rights), treating them on a par with our basic right to liberty. It's no accident that countries that privilege such "rights" are generally less free, often far less free, than those that don't. Fortunately, the United States has not yet ratified the international covenant on such rights.

36. I have discussed these issues more fully in Roger Pilon, "Freedom, Responsibility, and the Constitution: On Recovering Our Founding Principles," *Notre Dame Law Review* 68, no. 3 (1993): 507–47.

37. A question that often arises is whether laws authorizing such illegitimate powers, if enacted and upheld *pursuant to predetermined neutral legislative and judicial procedures*, are "good law." Many natural law proponents hold, for example, that positive law inconsistent with natural law is "no law at all." The better answer, I submit, is to recognize the distinction between the two, to acknowledge that legislators and judges make mistakes, and to abide by the positive law until it can be corrected or otherwise overturned.

2

HOW PLEA-DRIVEN MASS ADJUDICATION UNDERMINED AMERICANS' RIGHT TO A JURY TRIAL

CLARK NEILY

For depriving us in many Cases, of the Benefits of Trial by Jury:

Among the most readily abused powers of government is the ability to accuse someone of a crime and then prosecute, convict, and punish that person. Indeed, throughout history, the ability to initiate criminal prosecutions and impose punishments with the imprimatur of judicial legitimacy has been among the effective tools used by repressive regimes against perceived dissidents. At the same time, a well-functioning criminal justice system is necessary to reliably identify, proscribe, and fairly punish harmful behavior that threatens the very fabric of civil society.

The Founders were acutely aware of this dichotomy, and it is no accident that they devoted nearly half of the Bill of Rights to setting forth an exceptionally detailed framework for resolving criminal charges. And the crown jewel of that process—and indeed arguably the apotheosis of criminal adjudication throughout the ages—is the guarantee of a public and adversarial trial before an impartial jury of ordinary citizens.

Yet despite the central role juries were meant to play in the polity, they are now practically extinct on American soil. As a result, and utterly contrary to the Framers' design, ordinary citizens have virtually no personal involvement in the administration of criminal justice. Notably, the practical elimination of constitutionally prescribed jury trials was not accomplished through any conscious choice or legislative enactment, but rather through our gradual embrace of "plea bargaining." This informal and largely opaque process for resolving criminal charges was virtually unknown in early American history and is utterly inimical to the Founders' vision of an open and adversarial system for resolving criminal charges.

Criminal Law as a Tool of Oppression

The use of penal laws by English monarchs to exert control over nobles, clergy, dissidents, colonists, and countless others is sufficiently familiar that it requires little elaboration. Suffice to say that rather than wielding despotic power unilaterally, British kings and queens generally preferred to operate within the ambit of formal law by enlisting the legislative authority of Parliament and creating special adjudicative bodies like the Star Chamber to provide legal cover for their predations.

As the unaccountable exercise of power in North America became a point of growing friction between the colonists and their sovereign, a key grievance was the attempt to marginalize local adjudicative bodies by depriving American courts of jurisdiction over a wide variety of cases and transferring them to royal vice-admiralty courts. This practice infuriated the colonists, who correctly perceived it as a direct assault on democratic self-government.[1]

And although modern historical accounts tend to focus on economic regulations like taxes and trade restrictions, "it was the threat to self-government—the liberties of assemblies on the high end, and of juries on the low end—that [was] the most visceral concern animating American resistance," notes historian Guy Chet.[2] And although "historical discourse on the Revolution focuses not on juries, but on legislatures," many colonists considered the former more salient because "jury trials offered *practical* liberty and *direct* self-governance . . . while most people in Britain and the colonies were not eligible to vote, all were eligible to face prosecution."[3]

Of course, Americans' experience with government oppression and the use of criminal law as a tool of social control did not end with the signing of the Declaration of Independence or the ratification of the Constitution. Thus, for example, the notorious Alien and Sedition Acts were enacted in 1798, just a decade after the Founding; and in 1838, Missouri, followed by the remaining slave states, passed a law criminalizing abolitionist expression of any kind. Following the Civil War, penal codes were used to enforce Jim Crow–era segregation and keep formerly enslaved people in a state of constructive servitude by limiting their ability to travel, work, and seek employment, and also by sentencing them to hard labor—slave labor in effect—upon conviction for even minor offenses.[4] A century on, federal and state officials used criminal law to oppress marginalized groups such as gays and lesbians (punctuated by the 1969 Stonewall riots following police raids on gay bars in New York City); civil rights leaders like Martin Luther King, Jr.; and members of the so-called counterculture (whose affinity for illicit substances made them easy targets for prosecution).

Juries Were Meant to Be Our Primary Protection Against the Abuse of Criminal Law

Acutely aware of the chronic abuse of criminal law, the Founders devoted considerable attention to safeguarding against it. And the mechanism on which they primarily relied for that purpose was the jury trial. The notion that small groups of ordinary citizens working together in the context of a single prosecution could plausibly constrain an oppressive regime may seem quaint today, but that is partly because modern juries have been hobbled and neutered to the point where the institution itself is, in the words of Professor Akhil Reed Amar, "but a shadow of its former self."[5]

Perhaps not surprisingly, the Founding generation had a much different conception of the criminal jury and its proper role in society than most Americans do today. Contrary to the modern misconception of juries as purely fact-finding bodies, early Americans considered them to be political bodies whose role went well beyond deciding the outcome of particular cases. Thus, Alexis de Tocqueville described the early 19th-century jury as "first and foremost a political institution" and "a form of popular sovereignty."[6] As such, the criminal jury may be thought of both as a representative of the "lower house" of a bicameral judicial branch[7] and as a kind of "petit legislature" charged with preventing unjust convictions and the imposition of unjust punishments.[8]

This protective role was exemplified for colonial-era Americans by the trial of newspaper publisher John Peter Zenger, who was prosecuted for committing seditious libel against the royal governor of New York, William Cosby. Zenger was acquitted in 1735 by jurors who rejected the trial judge's instruction that they confine themselves to the question of whether Zenger himself had published the statements at issue and not consider either the accuracy of those statements or the legitimacy of the law that made it illegal to publish them.[9] This prototypical example of what came to be known as jury nullification was hailed by Founding-era Americans as a paradigmatic example of how jurors can protect fellow citizens from the abuse of criminal law.

The Founders' reliance on citizen juries as an antidote to government oppression is manifest both in the main body of the Constitution, which provides that the trial of all crimes shall be carried out by jury,[10] and in the Bill of Rights, which devotes more words to criminal procedure—with particular attention to jury trials—than to any other topic, and mentions juries in three separate amendments.[11]

Plea Bargaining, Coercion, and the Myth of the Purely Fact-Finding Jury

Today, we have largely abandoned the constitutionally prescribed process for resolving criminal charges in favor of plea-driven mass adjudication. Unknown at the Founding and nowhere mentioned in any state or the federal constitution, plea bargaining arose informally during the late 19th century as an easy way to decide cases without the expense and inconvenience of a jury trial.[12] With little oversight from the judiciary and none from legislatures, plea bargaining soon became the default mechanism for resolving criminal charges in America.

Thus, as Justice Anthony Kennedy observed in 2012, "Criminal justice today is for the most part a system of pleas, not a system of trials."[13]

Our modern reliance on plea bargaining to decide cases raises a host of legal, political, and moral concerns, including the use of coercion to induce trial waivers and the specter of false confessions. But before discussing these problems and how to address them, it is helpful to consider why the government has so easily displaced the criminal jury from its assigned role as a key democratic guardrail against government oppression.

The short answer is that the judiciary committed two fundamental mistakes in response to prosecutors' rationally self-interested pursuit of greater efficiency and certainty in the adjudicative process. In the first of those mistakes, judges embraced a false conception of the jury as a purely fact-finding body with no legitimate role in "second-guessing" legislative enactments; in the second, judges decided that, unlike confessions during police interrogations, courts should play no meaningful role in preventing prosecutors from using coercion to elicit guilty pleas. These fundamental errors simultaneously rendered the right to a jury trial less valuable to defendants and more costly for them to invoke—with entirely predictable results.

The process by which judges fundamentally transformed criminal juries by stripping away their injustice-preventing role is recounted in Clay Conrad's 1998 book, *Jury Nullification: The Evolution of a Doctrine*. More recently, the topic has been addressed in excellent law review articles by Aliza Plener Cover, University of Idaho dean of faculty and professor of law,[14] and by Chris Kemmitt, a director of the Legal Defense and Education Fund at the National Association for the Advancement of Colored People.[15] As Professor Cover explains, Founding-era juries "had a vast power to find both fact and law" together with "*de jure* authority" to ignore the instructions of judges. That freedom of action enabled them to "serv[e] as a potent communitarian check on government overreaching."[16] Similarly, Kemmitt notes, "When creating their own legal institutions, the colonists endorsed roles played by the English jury—namely, mitigator of unduly harsh sentences and populist check on a potentially unresponsive central government."[17] As an illustration of that role in action, Conrad notes, "Independent jury verdicts in Fugitive Slave Act cases"—that is, verdicts in favor of escaped slaves and against their purported owners—"were common enough that the federal judiciary regularly admonished jurors in such cases not to vote their consciences."[18]

But this conception of the jury as an injustice-preventing body started to change in the mid-19th century as state supreme courts began rejecting the idea that juries had any legitimate law-finding role—sometimes in direct contravention of state constitutional text.[19] In 1895, the Supreme Court officially embraced this view, holding in a 5–4 decision over vigorous dissents that "the law in criminal cases is to be determined by the court" and not by jurors.[20] From there, it was but a short step to our current approach, which is to limit criminal juries to a purely fact-finding role by removing potential jurors who express a belief in jury independence and by falsely advising those who serve that they would violate their oath as jurors if they rendered a verdict on the basis of any consideration other than the facts of the case and the law as provided to them by the judge.[21] Indeed, the Maryland Supreme Court recently told trial courts to instruct jurors that it is legally impermissible for them to acquit against the evidence,[22] which, as the dissenting opinion points out,[23] represents a blatant misstatement of the law[24] as well as centuries of Anglo-American practice.[25] By ignoring this history and transforming the criminal jury into a purely fact-finding body, courts ensure that, as Cover notes, "defendants who elect to exercise their right to a jury trial are offered a weakened version of that original right."[26]

Having thus devalued the constitutionally guaranteed right to a criminal jury trial, the government also substantially increases the cost of invoking that right by inflicting substantial trial penalties on defendants who go to trial and lose. In a 2018 report documenting this disturbing trend, the National Association of Criminal Defense Lawyers defines a "trial penalty" as "the substantial difference between the sentence offered prior to trial versus the sentence a defendant receives after a trial." The report also shows that defendants who exercise their right to trial routinely receive sentences three or four times longer—or even more—than those who plead guilty.[27]

But trial penalties are just the beginning. American prosecutors possess a fearsome array of tools with which they can—and routinely do—exert extraordinary pressure on criminal defendants to plead guilty.[28] Those tools include pretrial detention, mandatory minimum sentences, creative charge-stacking, and even threats to indict (or a promise not to indict) a defendant's family members—and are used simply to exert plea leverage.[29] These coercive levers are especially potent in the federal system, which helps explain why more than 97 percent of federal convictions are obtained from guilty pleas[30] and only 2 percent of cases end up going to trial.[31]

Although judges, prosecutors, and other system actors remain largely indifferent, the demonstrable use of coercion in plea bargaining raises serious questions of political and moral legitimacy. First and foremost, there is the so-called innocence problem—that is, the demonstrable fact that innocent people in our system regularly plead guilty to crimes they did not commit.[32] To take just one illustration, of the nearly 3,500 names on the National Registry of Exonerations, fully 18 percent pleaded guilty to crimes of which they were innocent.[33] And because law often makes it extremely difficult for people who have pleaded guilty to later challenge their convictions, there is little question that this represents merely the tip of the iceberg when it comes to the innocence problem.

Second, plea bargaining is so efficient that it enables the government to pursue vastly more prosecutions than it would if each one had to culminate in a jury trial. That includes cases of such marginal value that the government would surely drop them if the only alternative were to incur the expense and inconvenience of a trial.[34] This practice raises profound questions about overcriminalization and mass incarceration: If society is unwilling to pay for a trial—including requiring 12 people to take time away from their work and their families to sit on a jury for days, weeks, or even months—that seems like a fair indication that the conduct at issue does not merit the potentially life-destroying sanction of imprisonment.

Time and again, plea bargaining undermines the perceived legitimacy of the criminal justice system in various ways. Such ways include (a) enabling the government to conceal untold quantities of official misconduct, such as constitutional violations committed by police during their investigation and apprehension of the defendant;[35] (b) creating doubts about the validity of convictions obtained through potentially coerced pleas;[36] and (c) enabling perpetrators of despicable crimes like Jeffrey Epstein to receive vastly lower punishments than they deserve.[37]

Finally, plea bargaining greatly reduces opportunities for democratic participation by supplanting jury trials with a process controlled by prosecutors (whose interest in maintaining a high conviction rate skews the process against defendants). As noted earlier, for much of the nation's history, the participation in jury service was considered a fundamental civic activity, at least on par with—if not more important than—voting in elections. As Professor Andrew Guthrie Ferguson observes, "At the time of the Founding, jurors were not mere fact-finders, but equal participants in a constitutional structure of shared power," and "Some Founding Fathers *considered the right to serve as a juror more fundamental to their constitutional and political identity than the right to vote.*"[38] As recounted by Professor Ferguson, Thomas Jefferson averred, "Were I called upon to decide whether the people had best be omitted in the Legislative or Judiciary department, I would say it is better to leave them out of the Legislature."[39]

As Justice Kennedy explained in *Powers v. Ohio*, by providing an "opportunity for ordinary citizens to participate in the administration of justice," the jury trial "preserves the democratic element of the law."[40] But jury service is more than that. According to Professor Brian C. Kalt, juries represent "the essence of democratic self-government. Having a group of citizens decide who is guilty of a crime or liable for damages—as opposed to having elites decide—is perhaps the most feasible way to have cases decided by the community. For all their learning and training, judges—even elected ones—do not represent the community as well as a jury."[41]

Are Criminal Jury Trials Gone Forever?

Perhaps the most urgent question in light of the foregoing account of mass plea bargaining's near-total displacement of criminal jury trials is: Will the pendulum ever swing back from our current system of industrial-scale, transactional "McJustice" to the transparent, adversarial, and above all citizen-centric process that the Founders so carefully described and prescribed in the text of the Constitution? And the answer is, nobody knows for sure.

On the one hand, it is entirely possible that once the mass-plea-bargaining horse has left the barn, there is simply no way to turn back the clock. With its combination of efficiency, certainty, and ostensible reliability, the strong affinity that judges, prosecutors, and other key system actors have for plea bargaining is both rational and implacable. And there is an undeniable surface appeal of the inevitable refrain that the system would "grind to a halt" without plea bargaining—if that objection is taken to mean that without plea-driven mass adjudication, it would be impossible to process anywhere near the number of defendants through the system or to obtain anything like the number of convictions.

On the other hand, this is a country with a long history of criminalizing behavior that is not morally wrong and that many people wish to engage in—and will continue to engage in even when criminalized. Hence, there will always be a strong argument against prosecuting every single criminal offense, from relatively minor traffic infractions to (not particularly harmful) regulatory crimes covering everything from running a business to running for office. In other words, prosecutors can and should prioritize which cases they choose to pursue and ensure that their necessarily scarce resources are deployed against those crimes and criminals that pose the greatest threat to society. At the risk of understatement, our current criminal justice system falls well short of that ideal.

One of the few things the entire Founding generation appears to have agreed on was the indispensable role of juries in liberal democracies. As Alexander Hamilton wrote in *Federalist* no. 83, "The friends and adversaries of the plan of the convention, if they agree in nothing else, concur at least in the value they set upon the trial by jury; or if there is any difference between them it consists in this: the former regard it as a valuable safeguard to liberty; the latter represent it as the very palladium of free government."[42] Today, we have largely abandoned that ancient wisdom in favor of a proposition that the Founders would doubtless have considered both foolish and radical: namely, that instead of due process and jury trials, an equally effective—and much more efficient—way of resolving criminal charges is simply for the government to identify a suspect and then ask that person, "Did you do this crime?"

Whether it is still possible to resurrect criminal jury trials as the default mechanism for resolving criminal charges remains unclear. But few things would do more to restore public confidence in the integrity of the criminal justice system and help us rethink whether we truly want (and need) our country to be the world's leading incarcerator of human beings.

Notes

1. Guy Chet, "Was the American Revolution a Rich Man's War but a Poor Man's Fight?," *Starting Points Journal*, July 5, 2021.

2. Chet, "Was the American Revolution a Rich Man's War?"

3. Chet, "Was the American Revolution a Rich Man's War?" (emphasis in original).

4. See, for example, Tessa M. Gorman, "Back on the Chain Gang: Why the Eighth Amendment and the History of Slavery Proscribe the Resurgence of Chain Gangs," *California Law Review* 85, no. 2 (1997): 449–50.

5. Akhil Reed Amar, "The Bill of Rights as a Constitution," *Yale Law Journal* 100, no. 5 (1991): 1190.

6. Alexis de Tocqueville, *Democracy in America* (1835), trans. Arthur Goldhammer (Library of America, 2004), p. 313, quoted in Akhil Reed Amar, "The Bill of Rights as a Constitution," p. 104.

7. See Chris Kemmitt, "Function over Form: Reviving the Criminal Jury's Historical Role as a Sentencing Body," *University of Michigan Journal of Law Reform* 40, no. 1 (2006): 109.

8. Kemmitt, "Function over Form," pp. 103–4.

9. See, for example, *Crown v. John Peter Zenger*, 1735, Historical Society of the New York Courts.

10. U.S. Const. art. III, § 2, cl. 3.

11. U.S. Const. amends. V, VI, VII.

12. See, for example, George Fisher, "Plea Bargaining's Triumph," *Yale Law Journal* 109, no. 5 (2000): 857 (providing detailed account of the origins and development of plea bargaining in America).

13. *Lafler v. Cooper*, 566 U.S. 156, 170 (2012).

14. Clay S. Conrad, *Jury Nullification: The Evolution of a Doctrine* (Carolina Academic Press, 1998; Cato Institute, 2014); and Aliza Plener Cover, "Supermajoritarian Criminal Justice," *George Washington Law Review* 87, no. 4 (2019): 875.

15. Kemmitt, "Function over Form," p. 105.

16. Cover, "Supermajoritarian Criminal Justice," p. 885 and n.60.

17. Kemmitt, "Function over Form," p. 103.

18. Conrad, *Jury Nullification*, p. 82.

19. Conrad, *Jury Nullification*, pp. 94–96.

20. *Sparf v. United States* 156 U.S. 51, 87 (1895); and see Conrad, *Jury Nullification*, pp. 99–106 (discussing majority and dissenting opinions in *Sparf* and noting that Justice Harlan's majority opinion "in no way suggested eliminating the power of juries, sua sponte, to nullify the law").

21. See, for example, *Handbook for Trial Jurors Serving in United States District Courts* (Administrative Office of the United States Courts, 2003), p. 14 (advising jurors that "[t]he members of the jury are sworn to pass judgment on the facts in a particular case. They have no concern beyond that case. They violate their oath if they render their decision on the basis of the effect their verdict may have on other situations.")

22. *State v. Sayles*, 244 A.3d 1139 (Md. Court of Appeals 2021).

23. *State v. Sayles*, 1171–74 (Hotten, J., dissenting).

24. See, for example, *United States v. Kleinman*, 880 F.3d 1020, 1031 (9th Cir. 2017). ("It is well established that jurors have the *power* to nullify, and this power is protected by 'freedom from recrimination or sanction' after an acquittal") (emphasis in original).

25. For example, the Supreme Court has observed that any system in which the "the discretionary act of jury nullification would not be permitted . . . would be totally alien to our notions of criminal justice." *Gregg v. Georgia*, 428 U.S. 153, 199 n.50 (1976).

26. Cover, "Supermajoritarian Criminal Justice," p. 880.

27. National Association of Criminal Defense Lawyers, *The Trial Penalty: The Sixth Amendment Right to Trial on the Verge of Extinction and How to Save It* (National Association of Criminal Defense Lawyers, 2018).

28. Clark Neily, "A Distant Mirror: American-Style Plea Bargaining Through the Eyes of a Foreign Tribunal," *George Mason Law Review* 27, no. 3 (2020): 719.

29. See *United States v. Seng Chen Yong*, 926 F.3d 582, 591–92 (9th Cir. 2019) (collecting cases).

30. US Sentencing Commission, *2023 Sourcebook of Federal Sentencing Statistics*, Table 11.

31. John Gramlich, "Only 2% of Federal Criminal Defendants Go to Trial, and Most Who Do Are Found Guilty," Pew Research Center, 2019.

32. See Jed S. Rakoff, "Why Innocent People Plead Guilty," *New York Review of Books*, November 20, 2014. See also Neily, "A Distant Mirror," pp. 727–29.

33. National Registry of Exonerations, guiltypleaproblem.org.

34. For a fascinating discussion of how efficiency can be a bug rather than a feature in the administration of criminal justice, see Darryl K. Brown, "The Perverse Effects of Efficiency in Criminal Process," *University of Virginia Law Review* 100, no. 1 (2014): 183.

35. See, for example, Somil Trivedi and Nicole Gonzalez Van Cleve, "To Serve and Protect Each Other: How Police-Prosecutor Codependence Enables Police Misconduct," *Boston University Law Review* 100, no. 3 (2020): 916 (explaining that "one underreported consequence of plea bargaining is its tendency to whitewash police misconduct"). See also Martin A. Sibelli, "Police Brutality and Coercive Plea Bargaining—the Long Shadow of the Trial Penalty," *The Champion*, November 2021.

36. A particularly horrific illustration is the false conviction and subsequent exoneration of Troy Mansfield after he was coerced into falsely pleading guilty to abusing a child by prosecutors who knew from the beginning that there were serious doubts about every aspect of the case and who illegally concealed exculpatory notes and other evidence from the defense. Tony Plohetski, "A Life of Shame:

How Williamson County Prosecutor's 23-Year-Old Notes Exposed a Father's Wrongful Conviction," *USA Today*, November 15, 2019.

37. See, for example, Carissa Byrne Hessick, *Punishment Without Trial: Why Plea Bargaining Is a Bad Deal* (Abrams Press, 2021), pp. 156–59 (describing how plea bargaining enables sex offenders like Jeffrey Epstein to avoid responsibility for their crimes by pleading guilty to lesser—and sometimes entirely fictional—offenses).

38. See, for example, Andrew Guthrie Ferguson, "The Jury as Constitutional Identity," *University of California Davis Law Review* 47, no. 4 (2014): 1108–9 (emphasis added).

39. Ferguson, "The Jury as Constitutional Identity," p. 1109n13 (quoting Letter from Thomas Jefferson to the Abbé Arnoux (July 19, 1789), reprinted in *The Papers of Thomas Jefferson*, vol. 15, ed. J. P. Boyd (Princeton University Press, 1958), pp. 282–83.

40. *Powers v. Ohio*, 499 U.S. 400, 406–07 (1991).

41. Brian C. Kalt, "The Exclusion of Felons from Jury Service," *American University Law Review* 53, no. 1 (2003): 124 (internal quotation and citation omitted).

42. Alexander Hamilton, "The Judiciary Continued in Relation to Trial by Jury," *Federalist* no. 83, *New York Daily Advertiser*, July 1788.

3

THE SEVENTH AMENDMENT CIVIL JURY RIGHT AND AGENCY ADJUDICATION

THOMAS A. BERRY

For depriving us in many Cases, of the Benefits of Trial by Jury:

The Seventh Amendment guarantees the right to a jury trial "in Suits at common law." But respect for the right to a jury trial did not begin with the enactment of the Seventh Amendment in 1791; it can be traced back centuries further. As legal scholar Charles Wolfram has recounted, "the colonists were firmly of the opinion that trial by jury in civil cases was an important right of freemen."[1] The Framers understood that the right to a civil jury trial was rooted in the Magna Carta and was a vital check on state power.[2]

The colonists and their leadership never veered from their esteem for—and demand for—the trial by jury. Trial by jury was declared "the inherent and invaluable right of every British subject in these colonies."[3] The First Continental Congress demanded the "great and estimable privilege of being tried by their peers in the vicinage."[4] The "accustomed and inestimable privilege of trial by jury, in cases of both life and property" was listed as among those rights denied by the

Crown.[5] And the Declaration of Independence charged the king with "[d]epriving us in many cases, of the benefits of Trial by Jury."[6]

Americans were well aware of the tactics that government officials might use to avoid facing juries. In the years leading up to the Revolution, English colonial administrators attempted to subvert the right to a civil jury trial by trying cases in specialized courts called "vice-admiralty" courts. Colonial authorities would seize American ships under the pretext that they had violated customs and revenue measures and then try their cases in the vice-admiralty courts, without the benefit of a jury.[7] The notorious Stamp Act was also originally enforced via prosecution in the vice-admiralty courts.[8] These courts not only sat without juries, but also applied a presumption in favor of the government.

The vice-admiralty courts posed such a threat to the right of trial by jury that they were specifically identified by George Mason as a significant complaint against British rule. In a letter to the Committee of Merchants in London, Mason wrote that the British had "depriv[ed] us of the ancient Tryal, by a Jury of our Equals."[9] Mason wrote that vice-admiralty courts forced the colonists to "defend [their] property before a Judge . . . a Creature of the Ministry."[10] If the same cases were prosecuted in England against Englishmen, many would have been tried in front of a jury.[11]

Foreshadowing the power of modern administrative agencies to choose either district court litigation or agency adjudication, British authorities could bring customs cases in either common law courts or the vice-admiralty courts. But bringing cases outside of common law courts came with certain benefits for the government.[12] One example is that defendants in vice-admiralty courts did not have the same rights to a convenient venue as they had in the common law courts. The vice-admiralty court in Halifax, North Carolina exercised jurisdiction across the length of the colonies, from the Floridas to Newfoundland.[13] Thus, if customs officials were uncertain of success, they could bring a case in Halifax rather than in a more convenient location, thus requiring the defendant to either travel a long distance or suffer a default judgment. Those who could not afford the trip to Halifax lost their case and their property.

And again, like agency adjudications, the vice-admiralty courts did not give defendants sufficient procedural protections. Once a vice-admiralty court found probable cause, American shipowners were precluded from bringing a separate common-law action against the officials who had seized their ships for conversion (the common-law term for an unlawful taking of property), or to recover costs. Such actions were precluded even if their vessels were eventually held to have been wrongly condemned.[14] Vice-admiralty courts further imposed an extremely high bar for those trying to prove that their property had been taken.[15]

The protections afforded by juries were not just theoretical to America's Founders. The pre-Revolutionary era featured several famous examples of juries protecting individual liberty from government oppression. Decades before America's independence, a jury had acquitted Pennsylvania founder William Penn, who had been arrested for preaching in defiance of the Church of England.[16] The jury refused to convict Penn even after threats from the bench.[17]

Juries in the colonial era defended not just the right to freedom of religion but also the right to freedom of speech. One of the most stirring pre-Revolutionary episodes was the prosecution and subsequent jury acquittal of John Peter Zenger in 1734.[18]

Zenger was a printer in New York who was arrested and charged with seditious libel for his criticisms of the royal governor of New York, William Cosby.[19] On his arrival in New York, Cosby had unjustifiably sought a payment amounting to half the salary of the acting governor, who had served for a year before Cosby's arrival.[20] When the acting governor refused to pay, Cosby sued. The case ordinarily would have required a jury, but Cosby arranged for the New York Supreme Court to sit in equity to hear the case.[21]

Cosby's blatant corruption prompted an outraged Chief Justice Lewis Morris to dissent. Morris authored an opinion describing the dangers that arise when officials evade legal processes, an opinion which Zenger then publicized.[22] Governor Cosby then removed the chief justice, leading Zenger to publish yet another article criticizing the governor.[23] Zenger was then charged with seditious libel.[24]

The right to a jury trial loomed large throughout the case, both because Cosby had attacked it and because it was ultimately the jury that protected Zenger's rights. A grand jury refused to indict Zenger, but Cosby pressed on in his prosecution and pursued a course of action that did not require a grand jury's indictment.[25] Cosby had

Zenger's attorneys disbarred, but this unexpectedly benefited Zenger, because his new attorneys made the novel argument that truth should be a defense to libel. Even though such a legal defense did not then exist, the jury saw the fairness in this argument and refused to convict.[26] The trial thus reinforced the notion of juries as checks on executive power. Gouverneur Morris later called Zenger's case "the germ of American freedom, the morning star of that liberty which subsequently revolutionized America."[27]

The Zenger trial is often considered one of the inspirations for the First Amendment.[28] But the case was also an impetus for the Seventh Amendment's enshrining of the right to trial by jury, a right that the Framers knew would be an additional safeguard for other rights like freedom of speech.[29]

Precisely because juries were so effective at curbing excessive or arbitrary exercises of power, the British authorities frequently tried to evade them. In the Administration of Justice Act of 1774, which is considered one of the "Intolerable Acts" and thus a contributing factor to the American Revolution, the British provided for the transfer of trials between the colonies and England.[30] This assault on the institution of the jury allowed for a different grand jury, or petit jury, in a different land and deprived accused colonists of a jury of their peers. Similarly, the Quebec Act, sometimes included as one of the Intolerable Acts, extended the borders of Quebec and thereby expanded the geographical reach of French civil law, under which there was no jury trial right.[31]

In response, the Founding generation demanded a civil jury trial guarantee. The lack of a right to a civil jury trial in the original Constitution was nearly fatal to its ratification.[32] Anti-Federalists galvanized opposition to the Constitution due to its lack of a Bill of Rights, and its lack of a right to a civil jury trial in particular.[33] Both future Vice President Elbridge Gerry and Founding Father George Mason identified the absence of a provision guaranteeing civil jury trials as a major reason why neither signed the Constitution.[34] The Anti-Federalists' concern over civil juries became so intense that Alexander Hamilton dedicated all of Federalist No. 83 to assuaging their fears, telling readers that "[t]he friends and adversaries of the plan of the convention, if they agree in nothing else, concur at least in the value they set upon the trial by jury." The Anti-Federalists' demand ultimately was met, of course, in the form of the Seventh Amendment.

As the legal scholar Wolfram explained, the Anti-Federalists viewed the guarantee of a civil jury trial as "the protection of debtor defendants; the frustration of unwise legislation; the overturning of the practices of courts of vice-admiralty; the vindication of the interests of private citizens in litigation with the government; and the protection of litigants against overbearing and oppressive judges."[35] "Another important function of the civil jury, was to provide the common citizen with a sympathetic forum in suits against the government."[36] One pseudonymous writer suggested in the pages of the *Pennsylvania Packet* that "it was quite predictable that a 'lordly court of justice' sitting without a jury in the federal courts would likely be 'ready to protect the officers of government against the weak and helpless citizens.'"[37]

It was understood that the civil jury right would protect litigants in disputes between private citizens. But the core of the demand for the right focused on suits brought by the *government* against citizens. The Seventh Amendment ensured that when the government threatened the private rights of citizens—their lives, liberty, or property—it was to be held accountable to a jury in any situation when an Englishman would have had one under British common law.

But over the decades-long growth of the administrative state, matters that should rightly be decided by juries have instead come to be adjudicated within agencies.[38] Those executive branch agency procedures are no substitute for a jury trial. They deny defendants a trial before a petit jury—the constitutional requirement for adjudicating private rights.[39] In its place, agencies offer defendants an initial hearing before an administrative law judge (ALJ). But evidence suggests that an agency's ALJs feel pressure to rule in favor of the agency they work for.[40]

The history of the Securities and Exchange Commission (SEC) provides a case study in how jury rights were weakened over time. Originally, the SEC brought cases for alleged securities law violations by litigating in Article III courts with trial by jury. The original Securities Exchange Act of 1934 empowered the Commission to enforce violations of the new securities laws primarily by filing lawsuits against defendants in federal court.[41] Administrative proceedings, by contrast, could be used only to expel people from membership in the national securities exchanges that the Act directly regulated.[42]

Even as the SEC's powers and duties expanded over the next several decades, a defendant's right to the procedures guaranteed by the Seventh Amendment was largely preserved. Each time the Commission received new powers, those new powers were justified as closely tied to the Commission's oversight authority.[43]

Given these limited administrative powers and the fact that SEC-regulated respondents had arguably consented to such procedures,[44] the system remained largely consistent with the traditional boundaries of agency adjudication.[45]

Over the past four decades, however, agencies have pushed the constitutional boundaries. In the 1980s, for example, concerns over insider trading led to an expansion of the remedies that the SEC could exact via the courts as punishment for violating the law.[46] With the enactment of the Securities Enforcement Remedies and Penny Stock Reform Act of 1990 (known as the "Remedies Act"), the Commission's administrative adjudications could, for the first time, result in money penalties against SEC-regulated parties and permanent cease-and-desist orders against even *nonregulated* parties.[47]

In the wake of the 2008 financial crisis, however, Congress took an unprecedented leap. In the Dodd–Frank Wall Street Reform and Consumer Protection Act of 2010, Congress empowered the SEC to impose harsh quasi-criminal sanctions against any private citizen through its own administrative adjudications, with limited, after-the-fact review by a federal court of appeals as defendants' only recourse.[48] The Commission had sought this extraordinary power decades earlier, but Congress had declined to grant it "specifically because the [Commission] might be perceived to have an incentive to conduct more enforcement actions through its own administrative proceedings."[49]

The results were predictable. In the aftermath of Dodd–Frank, the SEC ramped up the number of cases it brought in its own in-house forums and amassed an impressive win rate before its own administrative law judges.[50]

The fear that such a scheme might come to pass is exactly the fear that motivated the Seventh Amendment. In SEC administrative adjudications, the deck is stacked heavily against the respondent from start to finish, with the burden of proof, as in the vice-admiralty courts of yore, effectively on the respondent rather than the government. That inverts where the burden rightly belongs.[51] As one former ALJ put it, "the burden was on the people who were accused to show that they didn't do what the agency said they did."[52]

This entire institutional arrangement embodies many of the worst-case-scenario arguments that the Anti-Federalists made for the indispensability of civil juries. The SEC arguably features unreliable adjudicators, reflexive deference to the government, and unilateral encroachment upon life, liberty, and property. At a time when our civil legal system now frequently imposes fines greater than those imposed for misdemeanors or even felonies,[53] the Seventh Amendment should resume its role as "an important right of freemen."[54]

Fortunately, there is strong evidence that the Supreme Court is moving us in the right direction. In *SEC v. Jarkesy*, the Supreme Court held that "the Seventh Amendment entitles a defendant to a jury trial when the SEC seeks civil penalties against him for securities fraud."[55] Based on the Supreme Court's reasoning, it is likely that other penalties inflicted by other agencies will likewise be held to trigger the right to trial by jury. As courts continue to move in that direction, we will draw closer to the system that the Framers originally envisioned.

Notes

1. Charles W. Wolfram, "The Constitutional History of the Seventh Amendment," *Minnesota Law Review* 57, no. 4 (1973): 654.

2. Wolfram, "The Constitutional History of the Seventh Amendment," p. 653n44; and Kenneth S. Klein, "The Validity of the Public Rights Doctrine in Light of the Historical Rationale of the Seventh Amendment," *Hastings Constitutional Law Quarterly* 21, no. 4 (1994): 1017.

3. Philip B. Kurland and Ralph Lerner, eds., *The Founders' Constitution* (University of Chicago Press, 1986), vol. 2, "Stamp Act Congress, Declaration of Rights."

4. Charles C. Tansill, ed., *Documents Illustrative of the Formation of the Union of the American States* (Government Printing Office, 1927), "Declaration and Resolves of the First Continental Congress," October 14, 1774.

5. Center for the Study of the American Constitution, University of Wisconsin-Madison, "Declaration of Causes and Necessity of Taking Up Arms of 1775."

6. National Archives, "Declaration of Independence: A Transcription," July 4, 1776.

7. Wolfram, "The Constitutional History of the Seventh Amendment," pp. 639, 654n47.

8. Danby Pickering, ed., *The Statutes at Large, from Magna Charta to the End of the Eleventh Parliament of Great Britain* (Joseph Bentham, 1765), vol. 26, chap. 12, "Stamp Act of March 22, 1765," LVII–LVIII.

9. "George Mason to the Committee of Merchants in London, June 6, 1766," *The Papers of George Mason 1725–1792*, vol. 1, ed. Robert A. Rutland (University of North Carolina Press, 1970), p. 65.

10. "George Mason to the Committee of Merchants in London, June 6, 1766."

11. Erwin C. Surrency, "Courts in the American Colonies," *American Journal of Legal History* 11, no. 3 (1967): 357.

12. American History Central, "Townshend Acts, Vice Admiralty Court Act Text," July 6, 1768; and Matthew P. Harrington, "The Legacy of the Colonial Vice-Admiralty Courts (Part I)," *Journal of Maritime Law and Commerce* 26, no. 4 (1995): 583.

13. Arthur J. Stone, "The Admiralty Court in Colonial Nova Scotia," *Dalhousie Law Journal* 17, no. 2 (1994): 380.

14. Wolfram, "The Constitutional History of the Seventh Amendment," p. 654n47.

15. Daniel D. Blinka, "Jefferson and Juries: The Problem of Law, Reason, and Politics in the New Republic," *American Journal of Legal History* 47, no. 35 (2005): 79.

16. Andrew R. Murphy, "The Emergence of William Penn, 1668–1671," *Journal of Church and State* 57, no. 2 (2015): 337.

17. Murphy, "The Emergence of William Penn," p. 339.

18. Wolfram, "The Constitutional History of the Seventh Amendment," pp. 654–55.

19. Wolfram, "The Constitutional History of the Seventh Amendment," pp. 654–55.

20. Walker Lewis, "The Right to Complain: The Trial of John Peter Zenger," *ABA Journal* 46, no. 1 (1960): 27.

21. Lewis, "The Right to Complain," p. 28.

22. Doug Linder, "The Trial of John Peter Zenger: An Account" (2001).

23. Lewis, "The Right to Complain," p. 30.

24. Lewis, "The Right to Complain," p. 30.

25. Lewis, "The Right to Complain," p. 29.

26. Lewis, "The Right to Complain," p. 111.

27. Linder, "The Trial of John Peter Zenger," p. 8.

28. Edward Bloustein, "The First Amendment 'Bad Tendency' of Speech Doctrine," *Rutgers Law Review* 43, no. 3 (1991): 509 (discussing the case as a "watershed in the evolution of freedom of the press") [quoting Leonard Levy, *Emergence of a Free Press* (Oxford University Press, 1985)].

29. Steven Alan Childress, "The First Amendment," *Texas Tech Law Review* 17 (1986): 626n66.

30. Pickering, *The Statutes at Large*, vol. 30, "Administration of Justice Act," May 20, 1774, pp. 367–71.

31. Pickering, *The Statutes at Large*, vol. 22, "Quebec Act," October 7, 1774, XI.

32. Klein, "The Validity of the Public Rights Doctrine," pp. 1017–20.

33. Wolfram, "The Constitutional History of the Seventh Amendment," p. 667; and *Parsons v. Bedford*, 26 U.S. (1 Pet.) 433, 446 (1830) ("One of the strongest

objections originally taken against the Constitution of the United States, was the want of an express provision securing the right of trial by jury in civil cases.").

34. Wolfram, "The Constitutional History of the Seventh Amendment," pp. 660n59, 667.

35. Wolfram, "The Constitutional History of the Seventh Amendment," p. 670.

36. Wolfram, "The Constitutional History of the Seventh Amendment," p. 708.

37. Wolfram, "The Constitutional History of the Seventh Amendment," p. 708.

38. *Granfinanciera, S.A. v. Nordberg*, 492 U.S. 33, 69 (1989) (Scalia, J., concurring) (protesting the rampant expansion of the "public rights" doctrine, which has permitted jury-free adjudication).

39. *Granfinanciera, S.A. v. Nordberg*, 492 U.S. 33, 69 (1989), 42.

40. Jean Eaglesham, "SEC Wins with In-House Judges," *Wall Street Journal*, May 6, 2015 (quoting a former ALJ as stating that she "came under fire . . . for finding too often in favor of defendants"); Charles H. Koch, Jr., "Administrative Presiding Officials Today," *Administrative Law Review* 46 (1994): 278–79 (finding that 34 percent of non–Social Security ALJs were "asked to do things that are against their better judgment," 15 percent believe "threats to independence were a problem," and 9 percent were "pressure[d] to make different decisions").

41. Thomas Glassman, "Ice Skating Up Hill: Constitutional Challenges to SEC Administrative Proceedings," *Journal of Business & Securities Law* 16 (2015): 50.

42. Glassman, "Ice Skating Up Hill," p. 50.

43. Glassman, "Ice Skating Up Hill," p. 50 (internal quotations omitted).

44. Stephen J. Choi and A. C. Pritchard, "The SEC's Shift to Administrative Proceedings: An Empirical Assessment," *Yale Journal on Regulation* 34 (2017): 6.

45. William Baude, "Adjudication Outside Article III," *Harvard Law Review* 133 (2020): 1554–57.

46. Glassman, "Ice Skating Up Hill," p. 51; and Ryan Jones, "The Fight over Home Court: An Analysis of the SEC's Increased Use of Administrative Proceedings," *SMU Law Review* 68 (2015): 511.

47. Paul S. Atkins and Bradley J. Bondi, "Evaluating the Mission: A Critical Review of the History and Evolution of the SEC Enforcement Program," *Fordham Journal of Corporate and Financial Law* 13, no. 3 (2008): 392–93; Jones, "The Fight over Home Court," pp. 511–12; and Choi and Pritchard, "The SEC's Shift to Administrative Proceedings," p. 7.

48. Choi and Pritchard, "The SEC's Shift to Administrative Proceedings," p. 9.

49. Jones, "The Fight over Home Court," p. 516 (internal quotations omitted).

50. Glassman, "Ice Skating Up Hill," pp. 56–57.

51. Compare *Patterson v. New York*, 432 U.S. 197, 211 (1977) ("[T]he universal rule in this country [is] that the prosecution must prove guilt beyond a reasonable doubt.").

52. Eaglesham, "SEC Wins with In-House Judges."

53. *Sessions v. Dimaya*, 138 S. Ct. 1204, 1229 (2018) (Gorsuch, J., concurring in part and in the judgment).

54. Wolfram, "The Constitutional History of the Seventh Amendment," p. 654.

55. *SEC v. Jarkesy*, 603 U.S. 109, 120 (2024).

4

A REVOLT AGAINST DISCRIMINATORY TAXATION

ADAM N. MICHEL AND JOSHUA LOUCKS

For imposing Taxes on us without our Consent:

The American Revolution was a tax revolt over consent; but it was also a rebellion against a system of taxation that was punitive, discriminatory, and enriching special interests on the other side of the Atlantic. Most historical accounts of taxation and the American Founding focus on the consent of the governed, starting and ending with the Declaration of Independence's grievance over "imposing Taxes on us without our Consent." Yet, this history glosses over a richer story of the Founding that has implications for fiscal systems today. If the taxes hadn't been arbitrary, punitive, and discriminatory, a revolt over consent may never have happened.

The pre–Revolutionary War period was punctuated by English imposition of various taxes (usually tariffs) designed not just to raise revenue but to preference commerce with Britain and assert at least notional control over the colonies. The colonists resisted these duties by boycotting taxed products and smuggling untaxed goods, but they still saw benefits from being part of the British Empire, such as military protection and access to credit. Fomented first by intentionally punitive measures in the Stamp Act and then the Tea Act, the colonists revolted, throwing the British East India Company's tea into Boston Harbor. Far from a revolt over taxes being too high, the colonists' Tea Party was in protest of a targeted *tax cut*. By exempting the British East India Company from taxes on tea, Parliament undercut domestic sellers, creating a tax-subsidized tea monopoly.

Following the revolutionary war, the nascent independent states were beset by their own internal tax revolts. Burdensome war debts meant the free colonies had to raise domestic taxes to pay bondholders. It was widely understood that government debt enriched wealthy urban elites who held the bonds. Taxes to fund the debt repayment fell disproportionately on poorer rural farmers, fomenting resentment and violent revolt in three early tax rebellions. Many protesters in these tax revolts went out of their way to ensure they were protesting the inequities of the tax design and not the principle of revenue raising in general.

This early American history demonstrates that people value not only low taxes but also nondiscriminatory fiscal systems. This tension played out in debates between the anti-Federalists and Federalist supporters of the new Constitution, which included language intended to ensure uniform treatment under the law, including the tax law. Unfortunately, these protections were insufficient to keep the anti-Federalists' warnings of an increasingly intrusive federal fiscal system from materializing. The Sixteenth Amendment and the introduction of the modern income tax exacerbated the inequities in the US tax system, most recently evident in tax legislation provisions favored by special interests, such as the Inflation Reduction Act's sprawling energy subsidies and the One Big Beautiful Bill Act's dozens of new or expanded tax preferences.

A Colonial Tax Revolt

From the founding of the American colonies, Britain sought to regulate trade to its benefit and raise revenue to fund the administration of the colonies. Taxes were imposed indirectly through trade restrictions and duties rather than via direct levies on the colonists.[1] However, as the British government's financial needs grew, especially after a series of costly wars, Parliament increasingly turned to direct taxation of internal commerce between the colonies. A series of taxes during the lead-up to the Declaration of Independence were designed to favor British economic interests and maintain control over the colonies. Punitive taxes such as those levied through the Stamp Act led to widespread resistance, including smuggling, boycotts, political protests, and, ultimately, a revolution.

British trade policy, which largely followed mercantilist ideas prevalent at the time, was designed to control colonial trade and enrich British interests by ensuring commerce flowed through the mother country. Many early laws were not targeted at the American colonies but imposed requirements that most colonial imports be carried on British and British colonial ships—to exclude rival imperial powers—and that certain valuable exports pass through British ports first before reaching their final destination.[2] These trade restrictions—and other laws, such as restrictions on harvesting colonial white pine trees and 100 percent duties on molasses—were widely ignored and spawned large-scale smuggling operations and pervasive black markets.[3]

Facing heavy debts following the end of the French and Indian War over control of North American territory (1754–1763), Parliament sought new sources of revenue from the American colonies through the Sugar Act of 1764.[4] The act lowered taxes on molasses (to decrease evasion and increase tax collections); expanded restrictions on traded goods, such as hides, skins, potash, and wine; enforced new fees and customs requirements on shipping; and strengthened British authority to seize smuggled goods and try smugglers in vice-admiralty courts, which denied colonists traditional English legal protections.

The following year, Parliament imposed the Stamp Act of 1765 as the first direct tax on internal transactions of items like legal documents, newspapers, and playing cards. These were unlike previous restrictions on trade, which, according to historian Alvin Rabushka, were understood to come "with the benefits of imperial protection, credit, and marketing arrangements. These benefits did not accrue from the Stamp Act, which was a revenue measure plain and simple."[5] Strong opposition to the new internal taxes led to widespread boycotts of British imports and the formation of the Stamp Act Congress, the first widely organized colonial protest against a British law. Before the Stamp Act, most colonists, especially elites, were content with British rule.[6] Opposition to the Stamp Act was widespread and not just led by elites, despite the tax disproportionately affecting merchants, lawyers, and printers.[7] Lynne Oats and Pauline Sadler argue that it was the poor design of the Stamp Act—specifically its requirement that paper be stamped in Britain and the active participation of the colonists—rather than the tax itself, that greatly contributed to the colonial distaste for the measure.[8] Colonial resistance, and the resulting loss of business for British merchants due to boycotts, quickly led to repeal of the law in March 1766.

However, Parliament did not concede its rights to tax the colonies. On the same day it repealed the Stamp Act, Parliament passed the Declaratory Act, which reasserted Parliament's right to tax and "to make laws and statutes of sufficient force and validity to bind the colonies . . . in all cases whatsoever."[9] In 1767, the Stamp Act was replaced with the Townshend Acts, which imposed duties on 72 items, including glass, paper, paint, lead, and tea. Renewed boycotts created economic disruptions on the other side of the Atlantic, which led Parliament to repeal all but the tea duty in March 1770. It retained the tax on tea to reaffirm its continued power to tax the colonists. By 1773, most of the British revenue in America came from the remaining duties on molasses and tea.

The Tea Act

The fateful Tea Act of 1773 was not another tax increase or expansion of taxing powers but a series of trade preferences given to the East India Company, which was in deep financial trouble at the time.[10] The British government used the Tea Act as a corporate bailout, allowing the East India Company to sell tea duty-free and bypass requirements to sell through English middlemen. The targeted tax cut allowed the company to sell tea in the American colonies at half its previous price, undercutting all competition, including competition from smugglers.[11] Like most government bailouts, this only temporarily saved the company from financial troubles.

And like many bailouts throughout history, it led to popular backlash. On December 16, 1773, a group calling themselves the Sons of Liberty boarded British ships and dumped 342 chests of tea into

Boston Harbor in protest. By that time, the Tea Act was widely seen as an attempt to establish British control over colonial commerce by providing a monopoly benefit to a politically connected corporation. Historians have interpreted this direct act of insurrection as a protest not against high tax burdens but against a tax break for the East India Company that undercut colonial competitors and reinforced corporate favoritism.[12] The British government retaliated with a series of punitive laws designed to punish Massachusetts for the Boston Tea Party and force colonial submission. Often called the Coercive or Intolerable Acts, these laws closed Boston Harbor, put Massachusetts under direct British rule, provided special legal protections for British officials, and allowed troops to be housed in private homes.[13] These acts backfired; instead of isolating Massachusetts, they led the colonies to unite against Britain, form the First Continental Congress, boycott all British goods, and declare independence on July 2, 1776, with final ratification two days later.

Notably, the colonial revolt was not over the fiscal burden placed on the colonies, which was not particularly high at the time.[14] Rather, the colonists rebelled over the *way* in which taxes were imposed on them, not the overall burden. As historian Niall Ferguson estimates, in 1763, the average British citizen paid about 26 shillings per year in taxes, compared to about 1 shilling per year for a New England colonist.[15] Similar estimates confirm that the colonists paid much lower overall tax burdens, including local taxes, than taxpayers on the other side of the Atlantic.[16] The low levels of tax that British authorities collected in the colonies covered only a fraction of the defense and other colonially provided services. Economists Sebastian Galiani and Gustavo Torrens observe that "unless the colonies believed that Great Britain would continue to subsidize their defense forever, independence, if anything, would force the colonies to collect more taxes to pay in full for their defense or face the consequences of a militarily weak state."[17]

Reiterating this dynamic in a speech to the British House of Commons, Edmund Burke criticized the Tea Act, arguing that Americans resisted taxation not because of the cost but because it violated their political rights. He warned that "the very folly and mischief of the act" was that it deliberately repealed the higher and more broadly applicable taxes "merely for the sake of insulting the colonies."[18] Burke argued that even small taxes, if poorly designed, could provoke political conflict and possibly war. He was proved right.

A Nation Founded on Equal Treatment Under the (Tax) Law

Taxation was at the heart of the American Revolution and remained a central concern in the founding of the United States. Among the grievances listed in the Declaration of Independence was King George III "imposing Taxes on us without our Consent." Many other grievances were complaints of unequal treatment and targeted retaliation under British rule. The Founders' writings show how consent of the governed is equally important as protections from discriminatory and oppressive government power.

The Founders' first attempt to codify these ideals was in 1781 under the Articles of Confederation. This system quickly proved challenging to operate in the young country as Congress lacked the power to raise revenue. Instead, the system relied on voluntary contributions from the states, which were often delayed or not paid at all.[19] This fiscal impotence undermined the legitimacy and functionality of the newly founded federal government.

To address these failures while preserving the principle of limited government, the Framers designed a more robust but carefully constrained taxing authority in the Constitution. The power to raise revenue was necessary to establish public credit, maintain national defense, and secure the rule of law, but it had to be exercised in a way that respected the balance between federal and state authority.[20] Structural protections such as the apportionment requirement for direct taxes and the uniformity clause for indirect taxes were written into the Constitution to guard against regional favoritism and economic oppression.[21]

As the fledgling republic's elected representatives debated the new Constitution, the issue of taxation—specifically, its fairness, uniformity, and potential for abuse—became one of the most vigorously contested points. Federalists insisted that these constitutional mechanisms, coupled with the system of representation and checks and balances, would be sufficient to prevent tax policy from becoming tyrannical or discriminatory. They viewed a central government with taxing power as essential for survival and stability.

The Anti-Federalists, wary of centralized power and opposing the new Constitution, feared that the federal government, without additional constraints, would simply mirror the British monarchy's worst abuses. In *Anti-Federalist No. 32*, Brutus warned of a federal taxing power so expansive that it could reach into every household and become oppressive. Echoing the Declaration of Independence, he warned of the risk of the government employing "a swarm of revenue and excise collectors" who would "prey upon the honest and industrious part of the community." He feared not just taxation, but taxation imposed unequally, falling heaviest on the poor and concentrating power in the hands of elites.[22]

While the Federalists supported the new Constitution and a strong central government, they, too, recognized the importance of tax fairness. In *Federalist* no. 36, Alexander Hamilton emphasized that the Constitution guarded carefully against abuses of the power to tax, emphasizing the requirement that "all duties, imposts, and excises shall be UNIFORM throughout the United States."[23] In *Federalist* no. 35, Hamilton further argued that limiting the federal government's taxing powers too narrowly to only taxes on imports would lead to "injurious excess."[24] Instead, a broader taxing power would lead to a more equal distribution of the tax burden and fewer economic distortions.

The Founders' emphasis on fairness in taxation was not an isolated concern but rather part of a broader commitment to equal treatment under the law, a foundational principle of the new republic. Historian Gordon Wood argues that the fear was not simply of taxation but of a government of the rich, by the rich, for the rich.[25] Both Federalists and Anti-Federalists feared the rise of arbitrary government power and viewed special privileges, whether economic or legal, as antithetical to the liberty for which they had fought. This commitment to equality was embedded in the Constitution via structural and substantive safeguards. The Fifth Amendment's due process clause ensures that no person may be deprived of life, liberty, or property without fair legal procedures, underscoring the requirement that the government treat all citizens equally before the law. Likewise, the privileges and immunities clause in Article IV prohibits states from favoring their residents over citizens from other states, reinforcing the principle of national legal equality. The commerce clause, too, was designed in part to prevent economic favoritism among states and to ensure uniform standards in trade and taxation. Of course, the Constitution's vision of equality coexisted with profound exclusions, most notably slavery and the denial of suffrage to women and men without property, that revealed the gap between ideals and reality.

Still, underlying these provisions was a shared belief that individual rights could only be secure within a legal framework committed to consistency and neutrality. Rights meant little if they could be selectively applied or withdrawn on the basis of geographic, political, or economic status. By codifying legal constraints on discrimination and favoritism, the Constitution sought to ensure that governmental power would be exercised not for the benefit of the few but according to universal principles of equality.

Commitment to equal treatment under the law also extended to the new federal taxation powers. The widely held concern that taxes could become oppressive, in both magnitude and design, led to key constitutional safeguards. Article I of the Constitution includes multiple provisions to constrain federal taxing power and ensure fairness. These include the requirement that direct taxes be apportioned among the states by population (Section 2); that revenue-raising bills originate in the House of Representatives, where the Founders believed political factions would protect against discriminatory taxes (Section 7); and that all duties and excises be uniform across the country (Section 8).[26] These mechanisms reflected the Founders' belief that taxation must be applied evenly and transparently, with proper political checks to prevent abuse.

Unfair Taxation: Tax Revolts in Early American History

The tension over taxes was not settled by the ratification of the Constitution and the attainment of representation. Instead, the nascent country's early history is punctuated by three significant tax rebellions—Shays's Rebellion, the Whiskey Rebellion, and Fries's Rebellion—over perceived inequities in the new tax systems. Taken together, these uprisings underscore how Americans remained deeply frustrated despite gaining representation. Their frustration often stemmed not from the existence of taxation itself but from its unequal application and concern over who benefited from federal expenditures.

The repeated pushback against selective taxation highlights an enduring principle of American governance: resistance to economic policies perceived as favoring narrow constituencies at the expense of ordinary citizens.

Shays's Rebellion (1786–1787)

After the American Revolution, the newly independent colonies imposed heavy taxes to pay off war debt.[27] In addition to high taxes, New England was suffering from an economic depression, and wealthy urban creditors demanded repayment of debts from rural farmers, many of whom were returning Revolutionary War veterans. This confluence of events disproportionately hurt small farmers who had their property seized and were jailed in debtors' prisons for failing to pay off taxes and loans.[28] To the impoverished farmers, such measures betrayed the liberty they had fought for, benefiting wealthy government creditors at the common people's expense.

Things could have been worse. As historian Woody Holton describes: "Even some Americans who wanted to extract more money from debtors and taxpayers acknowledged that taking too much could diminish their productivity. The Massachusetts legislature approved an unprecedented levy in March 1786 but decided against imposing an even higher tax on farmers out of fear that 'increasing the demands might rather tend to dishearten them, and to lessen those exertions, which were, in fact, within their power.'"[29]

After ignoring pleas for relief, a rebellion grew. One of its most famous leaders was Daniel Shays, a struggling farmer and former Continental Army captain. The rebellion was short-lived, put down by a local militia raised by Boston merchants, but it sent shockwaves through the young nation and is often cited as a key catalyst for the Constitutional Convention and the need for a stronger federal government and centralized taxing power. At the same time, Shays's Rebellion became a symbol of grassroots protest in the new republic.

Historian Robert A. Gross dubbed it "the mother of all populist insurgencies against government run in the interest of financial elites."[30]

Whiskey Rebellion (1791–1794)

Just two years following the ratification of the new Constitution, Treasury Secretary Alexander Hamilton advocated an excise tax on all distilled spirits, supposedly to raise revenue to pay back Revolutionary War–era debts. Hamilton chose a tax on spirits *because* it was unpopular and viewed as discriminatory against the rural frontier farmers who distilled and used whiskey as a store of value, often using it to pay wages or rent. Thus, it was a tax on their wages and savings, and they lacked the cash to pay the new levy. Hamilton anticipated and welcomed resistance to the whiskey tax, understanding it as likely provoking an uprising. Some scholars went so far as to say that "Hamilton was gunning for a confrontation with America's unruly backcountry" in order to prove the federal government's newly established power to tax.[31]

Resistance began almost immediately after the tax's passage in 1791. Farmers in western Pennsylvania harassed tax collectors, refused to pay, and sometimes resorted to violence, tarring and feathering officials and burning their homes. The unrest escalated into an outright rebellion in 1794 when over 500 armed men marched to the home of a federal tax inspector. On the four-mile march, the rebels stopped to amend their demands. They opposed the purposefully targeted tax on their livelihoods, but they amended the demand note to make clear that "the people did not refuse to pay a proportional part of the revenue."[32]

President George Washington mobilized 13,000 militia troops and ended the rebellion without major bloodshed. Hamilton succeeded at fomenting an uprising to demonstrate the new power of the federal government to lay and collect taxes. The Whiskey Rebellion is usually juxtaposed with Shays's Rebellion, as demonstrating the strength of the new constitutional system. The underappreciated story is that it was not simply another tax revolt but a revolt over a tax designed to be discriminatory and perceived—correctly—as targeting the livelihoods of rural frontier farmers. This was the same complaint lodged by the Boston Tea Partiers. In all three cases, Americans showed their disdain for unequal and selective taxation.

Fries's Rebellion (1799–1800)

Just a few years later, German American farmers in eastern Pennsylvania resisted a new federal tax on property imposed by President John Adams's administration. The Direct Tax of 1798 was meant to raise funds for a potential conflict with France. It required assessments on land, houses, and slaves, which disproportionately affected rural Pennsylvania farmers, many of whom were already struggling economically. The tax was particularly unpopular because it included detailed inspections of homes to assess their value, which many farmers saw as an invasion of privacy and a form of government overreach. The tax also fell particularly hard on rural farmers whose lands and possessions were subject to foreclosure.

Like the tax revolts before it, the rebellion led by John Fries, a veteran of the Revolutionary War, was animated not so much by the tax itself, but by its perceived unfairness. In that sense, Fries's Rebellion underscored the deep resentment among rural farmers toward federal taxation and government authority, particularly when it appeared to favor wealthier coastal elites over working farmers. It was, as described by historian Terry Bouton, "a popular challenge to a system of government that routinely favored the interests of the elite at the expense of ordinary citizens."[33] The rebellion was short-lived, however, as President Adams dispatched federal troops to put down the rebellion and restore order.

Drawing on this history in his farewell address as president, George Washington warned that while taxes are necessary, the "selection of the proper objects" to tax is a politically perilous question. Despite difficulties in designing perfect taxes, Washington called "for a spirit of acquiescence" to unpopular taxes.[34] His speech underlines the lessons from events leading up to the Declaration of Independence and the three early American tax revolts: It is not necessarily the need for revenue but a tax's design and unequal burden that is often the spark that ignites the fire of revolution. Equal treatment under the law is an enduring American principle that cannot be overlooked in any aspect of governance, especially in an issue as burdensome as taxation.

Revenge of the Anti-Federalists and the Modern Income Tax

The repeated revolts against taxes that were perceived to be punitive and targeted lit the fire of the American Revolution and profoundly shaped the early republic. Shays's Rebellion provided fodder for those who wanted a stronger central government to call the Constitutional Convention, which gave Washington and Adams the powers they needed to crush similar uprisings. Tensions over taxes did not disappear with independence; instead, they evolved alongside the nation's tax system, reemerging in new forms as the fiscal systems expanded and became more complex.

As the new federal government sought stable revenue sources, it turned primarily to tariffs. These duties on imported goods provided the bulk of federal income throughout the 19th century and were seen as a more politically palatable form of indirect tax. Tariffs also appealed to Federalists like Hamilton as a tool for economic development, since he believed they helped protect fledgling American industries against foreign competition. But periods of high protective tariffs were often short-lived and fraught with controversy.[35] The 19th century saw repeated clashes between tariff advocates in manufacturing-heavy regions and tariff opponents in agricultural and other trade-reliant areas, culminating in major political ruptures like the Nullification Crisis of 1832.[36]

These conflicts reinforced the lesson that even indirect taxes could become flashpoints when they were perceived to favor one group over another. Growing dissatisfaction with the corruption and inequities of the tariff system eventually led to the adoption of the income tax in the 20th century—a shift that promised a fairer, more transparent, and less easily manipulated approach to federal taxation.[37] However, the income tax not only failed to deliver on that promise, it led to today's complicated and byzantine tax code and the special interest lobbying around it.

The introduction of the federal income tax in 1913 marked a turning point, fundamentally changing how Americans are taxed. Perhaps informed by the memory of early tax revolts, officials originally designed the income tax as a "class tax," targeting the highest-income one percent of earners and overturning the Federalists' promise of uniform tax burdens. Over time, the income tax expanded incrementally, first as top tax rates were raised and then as the tax base was broadened to include more middle-class earners.

The income tax and automatic withholding enabled a dramatic expansion of the federal government, giving credence to the Anti-Federalist warnings that federal tax powers "to provide for the general welfare" would be interpreted too broadly, allowing the federal fiscal system to encroach on every aspect of private life. As the Anti-Federalists feared, such unchecked fiscal authority "must necessarily, from its very nature, swallow up all the power of the state governments" and intrude into every aspect of the private economy.[38]

French Enlightenment philosopher Voltaire warned that in monarchical systems, the wealthy and politically connected "nobles, clergy, and government officials" often escape taxation, shifting the burden onto the poor, working classes.[39] Today, a different imbalance has emerged. While the overall tax burden is considerably higher than it was in the Founding era, federal taxes fall disproportionately on higher earners, while a growing share of the population pays little or nothing. On average, the lowest income, 20 percent of Americans, face negative effective tax rates and are net beneficiaries of the tax system.[40] This inversion has fueled a tax code increasingly shaped by political bargaining by higher-income constituencies and business interests, filling the tax code with preferences, loopholes, and exemptions that distort economic incentives and foster resentment of an opaque system open to manipulation.

Across the political spectrum, concerns about inequality in the application of the fiscal system continue to fuel grassroots movements, such as Occupy Wall Street on the left and the Tea Party on the right. Both reflect frustration with a system seen as rigged to benefit the powerful at the expense of ordinary Americans. Many Americans, despite having formal political representation in Washington, remain dissatisfied with the fiscal system for the same two reasons the Founding Generation gave: The overall fiscal burden has grown significantly, hindering wealth-building and independence, and the tax system has become a tool of political favoritism.

Recent laws, such as the Inflation Reduction Act, the CHIPS Act, and the One Big Beautiful Bill Act, exemplify this dynamic. Each bill grants tax incentives to favored industries and constituencies while increasing compliance costs and direct tax burdens on others.[41] Much like the 1773 Tea Act, which granted the British East India Company special tax treatment at the expense of colonial merchants, these modern laws use the tax code as an instrument of economic privilege and punishment.

As the Anti-Federalists warned, unchecked federal taxing power risks not only excessive taxation but also the creation of a patronage state, where government selectively rewards politically aligned constituencies. While modern Americans enjoy representation, the core grievances that fueled the American Revolution—unequal treatment under the law, particularly tax laws—persist.

The challenge today is not simply to lower taxes but also to design a system that is transparent, neutral, broad-based, and resistant to political manipulation. Voters and policymakers alike should revisit the warnings of the Anti-Federalists and the animating grievances of the Founding Generation. Throughout American history, the people have resisted systems of taxation that disproportionately benefit the powerful, whether it was the East India Company in 1773 or politically connected industries today. To restore trust and encourage prosperity, taxation must once again reflect the nation's foundational commitment to equal treatment under the law.

Notes

1. Neil S. Siegel and Steven J. Willis, "Direct and Indirect Taxes," National Constitution Center.
2. An Act for Increase of Shipping, and Encouragement of the Navigation of This Nation, Parliament of England, 1651; An Act for the Encouraging and Increasing of Shipping and Navigation, Parliament of England, 1660; and An Act for the Encouragement of Trade, Parliament of England, 1663.
3. The White Pines Acts placed specific restrictions on harvesting white pines, reserving the New England forests for the king. The Molasses Act of 1733 imposed a heavy tax on non-British molasses, sugar, and rum to protect West Indian plantations. With lax enforcement and high rates, the taxes did not raise much revenue for the crown. Alvin Rabushka, *Taxation in Colonial America* (Princeton University Press, 2008), p. 736.
4. Sebastian Galiani and Gustavo Torrens, "Why Not Taxation and Representation? British Politics and the American Revolution," *Journal of Economic Behavior and Organization* 166 (2019): 28–52.
5. Rabushka, *Taxation in Colonial America*, p. 744.

6. Adam E. Zielinski, "Life in Colonial America Prior to the Revolutionary War," American Battlefield Trust, July 24, 2024.

7. Edmund S. Morgan and Helen M. Morgan, *The Stamp Act Crisis: Prologue to Revolution* (University of North Carolina Press, 1995).

8. Lynne Oats and Pauline Sadler, "Accounting for the Stamp Act Crisis," *Accounting Historians Journal* 35, no. 2 (2008): 101–43.

9. An Act for the Better Securing the Dependency of His Majesty's Dominions in America upon the Crown and Parliament of Great Britain, Parliament of Great Britain, 1766.

10. Avik Roy, "Bad Economics and Bank Bailouts Were the Norm Long Before TARP: A Retrospective on the East India Company," *Forbes*, April 14, 2013.

11. Rabushka, *Taxation in Colonia America*, p. 747; and T. H. Breen, *The Marketplace of Revolution: How Consumer Politics Shaped American Independence* (Oxford University Press, 2005).

12. Breen, *The Marketplace of Revolution.*

13. Caroline Eisenhuth, "The Coercive (Intolerable) Acts of 1774," George Washington's Mount Vernon.

14. Caleb Petitt, "What the American Colonies Teach Us About Tax Competition," *The Unseen and the Unsaid* (blog), April 21, 2025.

15. Galiani and Torrens, "Why Not Taxation and Representation?," pp. 28–52; and citing Niall Ferguson, *Empire: The Rise and Demise of the British World Order and the Lessons for Global Power* (Basic Books, 2004).

16. Gary M. Walton and James F. Shepherd, *The Economic Rise of Early America* (Cambridge University Press, 1979); Rabushka, *Taxation in Colonial America*; and Woody Holton, *Liberty Is Sweet* (Simon & Schuster, 2021).

17. Galiani and Torrens, "Why Not Taxation and Representation?," p. 32.

18. Edmund Burke, *The Works of the Right Honourable Edmund Burke*, vol. 2 (1887; Project Gutenberg, 2006).

19. Michael Hattem, "Newburgh Conspiracy," George Washington's Presidential Library at Mount Vernon, March 26, 2025.

20. Jared Walczak, "How Failed Tax Policy Led to the Constitutional Convention," Tax Foundation, September 16, 2016.

21. Siegel and Willis, "Direct and Indirect Taxes"; and U.S. Const. article I, § 8, cl. 1.

22. *The Anti-Federalist Papers*, no. 32 (Brutus) (The Constitutionalist Society, 2017).

23. *The Federalist Papers*, ed. Clinton Rossiter, no. 36 (Alexander Hamilton) (New American Library, 1961), pp. 217–23 (capitalization in original text).

24. *The Federalist Papers*, ed. Clinton Rossiter, no. 35 (Alexander Hamilton) (New American Library, 1961), pp. 211–17.

25. Gordon S. Wood, *The Creation of the American Republic, 1776–1787* (University of North Carolina Press, 2006).

26. U.S. Const. article I.

27. Thomas Ladenburg, "Paper Money and Shays' Rebellion," *Digital History*, 2007.

28. Bill of Rights Institute, "Shays' Rebellion."

29. Woody Holton, "Did Democracy Cause the Recession That Led to the Constitution?" *Journal of American History* 92, no. 2 (September 2005): 463.

30. Robert A. Gross, review of *Shays's Rebellion: The American Revolution's Final Battle*, by Leonard L. Richards (University of Pennsylvania Press, 2002), *New England Quarterly* 76 (March 2003): 126.

31. Vanessa Williamson, "The Whiskey Rebellion and the Fight for Equal Taxation in Early America," Tax Policy Center, December 15, 2021, p. 4; citing Philip Sheldon Foner, *The Democratic-Republican Societies, 1790–1800: A Documentary Sourcebook of Constitutions, Declarations, Addresses, Resolutions, and Toasts* (Greenwood Press, 1976), p. 28; and Ray Tyler, "The Whiskey Rebellion," Teaching American History, January 12, 2021.

32. Trial transcript of *United States vs. Robert Porter*, MFF 2739, Library and Archives Division, Senator John Heinz History Center, Historical Society of Western Pennsylvania, quoted in Terry Bouton, *Taming Democracy* (Oxford University Press, 2007); Williamson, "The Whiskey Rebellion"; citing Bouton, *Taming Democracy*, p. 233.

33. Terry Bouton, "'No Wonder the Times Were Troublesome': The Origin of Fries Rebellion, 1783–1799," *Pennsylvania History* 67, no. 1 (Winter 2000): 24.

34. United States Senate Historical Office, "Washington's Farewell Address," 1796.

35. Joseph Bishop-Henchman, "High Protective Tariffs Have Been Short-Lived in American History," *Cato at Liberty* (blog), Cato Institute, April 8, 2025.

36. "Nullification Crisis," American Battlefield Trust.

37. Phillip Magness, "A Club to Beat Down the Tariff: The Political Economy of Tax Swaps and the Interest Group Origins of the 16th Amendment," Independent Institute, May 8, 2016.

38. *The Anti-Federalist Papers*, no. 32 (Brutus).

39. He notes that these unequal taxes were "a fuse to the fire of the Great Revolution." Voltaire, *Voltaire in His Letters, Being a Selection from His Correspondence*, translation S. G. Tallentyre (G. P. Putnam's Sons, 1919), chap. "A Plea for the Poor, To M. de Farges."

40. "Distribution Table: 2024 001: Distribution of Families, Cash Income, and Federal Taxes Under 2023 Current Law," Office of Tax Analysis, Department of Treasury, October 30, 2023.

41. Travis Fisher and Joshua Loucks, "The Budgetary Cost of the Inflation Reduction Act's Energy Subsidies: IRA Energy Tax Credits Could Cost $4.7 Trillion by 2050," Cato Institute Policy Analysis no. 992, March 11, 2025; Adam Michel, "Republicans' One, Big, Beautiful Tax Bill Needs a Makeover," *Cato at Liberty* (blog), Cato Institute, May 14, 2025; and *Hearing on Made in America: The Boom in U.S. Manufacturing Investment, Before the Joint Economic Committee*, 118th Cong. (2024) (statement of Scott Lincicome, vice president of General Economics and Stiefel Trade Policy Center at the Cato Institute).

5

THE FOUNDERS' POLICY OF FREE IMMIGRATION

DAVID BIER

He has endeavoured to prevent the population of these States; for that purpose obstructing the Laws for Naturalization of Foreigners; refusing to pass others to encourage their migrations hither, and raising the conditions of new Appropriations of Lands.

America's traditional immigration policy was one of free immigration. America's Founders believed that the United States should be, as George Washington put it, "open to receive not only the Opulent and respectable Stranger, but the oppressed and persecuted of all Nations and Religions."[1] He also wrote that he "always hoped that this land might become a safe and agreeable Asylum."[2] This idea of an American "asylum"—a place for freedom in a world of tyrannies—formed the basis of the Founders' views on immigration even before they achieved independence. In *Common Sense*, the 1776 pamphlet that inspired the Revolution, Thomas Paine called for America to become an "asylum for mankind."[3] Samuel Adams rallied Bostonians by reiterating the line later that year: "Our contest is not only whether we ourselves shall be free, but whether there shall be left to mankind an asylum on earth for civil and religious liberty."[4]

Following the natural rights philosophers of the time, the Declaration of Independence outlined the rights to life, liberty, and the pursuit of happiness as coming from God, not from citizenship or immigration status granted by governments.[5] To the Founders, every person was born naturally free, and the government's only legitimate function was to protect that freedom. In *A Summary View of the Rights of British America*, effectively the 1774 prelude to the Declaration, Thomas Jefferson described emigration as a fundamental expression of that freedom: "a right which nature has given to all men, of departing from the country in which chance, not choice, has placed them, of going in quest of new habitations."[6] After the colonies gained their independence, Jefferson believed it was "fortunate for the United States to have become an asylum."[7]

Free immigration was a central principle for the Founders. The Declaration of Independence lamented how Parliament was "obstructing the Laws for Naturalization of Foreigners; refusing to pass others to encourage their migrations hither."[8] In 1783, as he negotiated the peace with Great Britain, John Adams foresaw economic crises in Europe that would "drive great Numbers to our Country," but wrote, "It is our Business to render our Country an Asylum, worthy to receive all who may wish to fly to it."[9] At the Constitutional Convention, the delegates agreed on "opening a wide door" (George Mason) to "great numbers" (James Madison).[10] They did not see their open door as a narrow funnel for elites.[11] Benjamin Franklin expressed concern about including anything in the Constitution that would even indirectly "discourage the common people from removing to this Country."[12] In 1791, Alexander Hamilton, articulating the economic policy for the new United States during the Washington administration, stated: "To find pleasure in the calamities of other nations would be criminal, but to benefit ourselves by opening an asylum to those who suffer in consequence of them is as justifiable as it is politic."[13]

The Founders expected America to welcome, as Washington said, people from "all Nations and Religions."[14] The new Constitution permitted immigrants to naturalize and even become judges or members of Congress, yet it banned any religious tests for holding public office, expecting that immigrants would run for office. Jefferson saw that American liberty would bring "within the mantle of its protection, the

Jew and the Gentile, the Christian and Mahometan, the Hindoo, and infidel of every denomination."[15] Declaration of Independence signer Richard Henry Lee argued, "True freedom embraces the Mahomitan and the Gentoo" (Hindu).[16] Franklin clearly articulated the implications for immigration. "Even if the Mufti of Constantinople were to send a missionary to preach Mohammedanism to us," he wrote, "he would find a pulpit at his service."[17]

This was not a begrudging "tolerance," said Washington, but rather, "*happily* the Government of the United States . . . gives to bigotry no sanction, to persecution no assistance."[18] The Founders gave life to the libertarian belief that the marketplace of ideas was the best path to the truth. James Madison, defending the Constitution in the Federalist Papers, argued that a larger and more diverse country with a "greater variety of parties and interests" would best safeguard liberty from factions "adverse to the rights of other citizens." For this reason, the Constitution limited government powers over anyone, and the Bill of Rights protected the rights of all "persons," not just citizens.[19]

The Founders were so universally in favor of free immigration that their debates were concentrated on how much to encourage it. At the Constitutional Convention, the delegates focused not on whether to allow immigrants to enter the country but on how quickly immigrants could enter Congress.[20] James Wilson of Pennsylvania, who helped produce the first draft of the Constitution, was himself an immigrant from Scotland and raised the possibility of his "being incapacitated from holding a place under the very Constitution which he had shared in the trust of making."[21] Ultimately, they settled on waiting periods of seven and nine years for the House and Senate, respectively. One in 10 members of the first Congress of the United States were immigrants—the highest proportion in American history.[22]

As the Declaration notes, a few colonies had implemented policies to encourage immigration, primarily through tax breaks that Parliament had blocked.[23] Some of the Founders, like Alexander Hamilton, wanted to cover immigrants' travel costs more directly.[24] However, most Founders followed George Washington's opinion that "except of useful mechanics—and some particular descriptions of men—or professions—there is no need of extra encouragement" for people to come.[25] Some Founders worried about immigrant assimilation, yet they did not support government intervention to limit immigration. Benjamin Franklin famously expressed reservations about German settlements in the 1750s, believing German culture was inferior.[26] But he still believed population growth and immigration benefited the United States economically, and he emphasized, "I am not against the Admission of Germans," declaring that they "contribute greatly to the improvement of a Country" and needed only to be integrated into English society.[27] By the 1780s, he listed Germans among the "multitudes of poor people" who had succeeded in the United States.[28]

In 1785, Jefferson also explicitly favored population growth and immigration but likewise questioned the "present desire of America . . . to produce rapid population by as great importations of foreigners as possible" because of worries that too many newcomers could overwhelm English culture. Nonetheless, he concluded, "If they come of themselves, they are entitled to all the rights of citizenship: but I doubt the expediency of inviting them by extraordinary encouragements" (i.e., tax breaks or subsidies).[29] By 1798, Jefferson had relinquished his doubts about immigrants' ability to assimilate and was denouncing proposals to strip immigrants of their rights and deport them without due process.[30]

As president, Jefferson welcomed immigrants and shortened the period required for naturalization. In a key passage from his 1801 inaugural address that was not lost on his critics,[31] he directly refuted his former concerns:

> Shall we refuse the unhappy fugitives from distress that hospitality which the savages of the wilderness extended to our fathers arriving in this land? Shall oppressed humanity find no asylum on this globe? The constitution, indeed, has wisely provided that, for admission to certain offices of important trust, a residence shall be required sufficient to develop character and design. But might not the general character and capabilities of a citizen be safely communicated to every one manifesting a bona fide purpose of embarking his life and fortunes permanently with us?[32]

The Founders saw no contradiction in expressing concerns about certain aspects of immigration while believing these issues could be addressed without the government restricting legal entry. They had learned from experience that the United States benefited from its welcoming policy.

The Period of Free Immigration Propelled America to Unprecedented Prosperity

The Founders' immigration policy was possibly the most successful economic policy ever adopted in American history. Allowing free immigration facilitated legal entry and population growth on an unprecedented scale, which generated enormous economic growth and prosperity.

Initially, a series of European and American wars kept immigration low from 1776 to the 1820s. However, after peace and with the introduction of steam-powered ocean liners in the 1830s, people immigrated at unprecedented rates.[33] In the 1850s, immigrants' share of the US population rose faster than in any decade in history, from less than 10 percent to more than 13 percent.[34] The legal immigration rate reached an unprecedented 1.6 percent of the US population—proportionally equivalent to nearly 5.5 million people today—entering as new immigrants in 1854 (Figure 1).[35] Immigrants represented between 13 and 15 percent of the population continuously from 1860 to 1920, and would have represented more if not for the fact that the second and third generations were being born so quickly.

That rapid increase in population fueled rapid economic growth. Immigrants, in fact, were indispensable to the US industrial revolution and built America's industrial centers. Since immigrants largely avoided the pre-civil rights South, they composed much higher shares of the population in states in other regions. In 1870, immigrants made up one in three residents of the West, and in 1910, they accounted for more than one in four people in the Northeast.[36] In cities, the immigrant concentration was even more pronounced. During the 19th century, immigrants became, at various times, roughly one-half of the residents of New York, San Francisco, Detroit, Chicago, Milwaukee, St. Louis, Cincinnati, New Orleans, and many other American cities.[37] Immigrants and their children formed overwhelming majorities in these cities. In the 19th century, American cities were essentially immigrant cities.

Figure 1

The legal immigration rate never recovered from the restrictions in the 1920s

Immigrants becoming legal permanent residents, share of population, 1820–2023

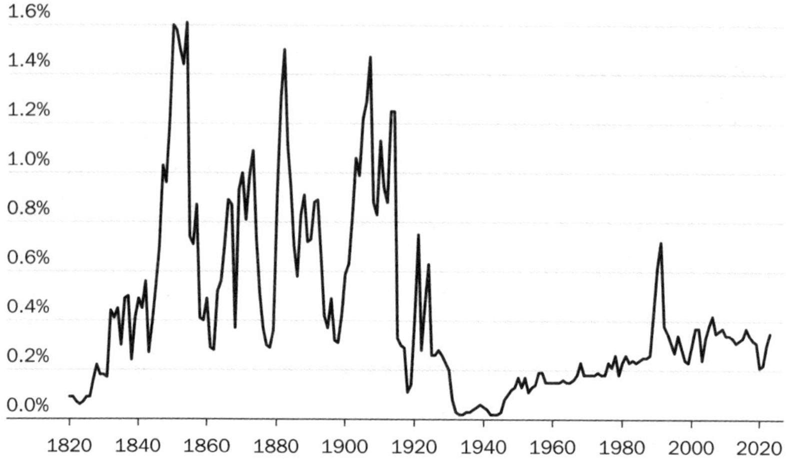

Source: Department of Homeland Security, "Yearbook of Immigration Statistics," 2022.

And it wasn't just in the cities. Chinese immigrants, who were about 90 percent of the Central Pacific Railroad construction workforce in the West,[38] were pivotal in helping the railroad overcome its early financial challenges, effectively serving as the railroad's "salvation," according to historian Richard White.[39] Similarly, Irish immigrants played a vital role in the Union Pacific Railroad.[40] By 1920, immigrants and their children made up half of all mining, construction, and manufacturing workers.[41] About 70 percent of Henry Ford's automobile assembly line workers were either immigrants or the children of immigrants.[42] Industrial manufacturing could not have occurred at scale without immigrants and their children acting as producers and consumers of the manufactured products.[43]

Immigrants and their children also helped drive 19th-century American innovation. Immigrants Alexander Graham Bell, from Scotland, and Antonio Meucci, from Italy, independently invented telephones. Scottish immigrant Andrew Carnegie revolutionized the steel industry, radically reducing the cost of steel production in the United States. Levi Strauss from Germany and Jacob Davis from Latvia invented denim jeans. Among other things, the Austrian immigrant Nikola

Tesla invented the alternating current system of transmitting electricity over long distances. John Augustus Roebling, from Germany, designed the then-largest and longest suspension bridges in the world, including the iconic Brooklyn Bridge. John Ericsson, from Sweden, invented the screw propeller for steamships. German immigrant Charles Pfizer pioneered the US pharmaceutical industry.

Thus, it is no exaggeration to say that immigration made America the world's largest economy. At the start of the 19th century, the United States did not rank among the world's largest economies. From 1830 to 1930, however, 38 million immigrants arrived in the United States, propelling rapid population growth in America from just 13 million in 1830 to over 123 million in 1930.[44] Immigrant-fueled population growth helped propel economic growth. US real GDP increased nearly 50-fold from 1820 to 1920.[45] As a result, just before the dawn of the 20th century, the United States became the world's largest economy for the first time.[46]

Immigration-fueled industrialization led to many of the most critical advancements in the standard of living of ordinary people throughout world history. America's immigrant cities were among the first in the world to implement modern sewage and water systems. Immigrant workers laid electrical power lines and pioneered mass transit.[47] This period saw the steepest decline in American history in the number of hours the average worker needed to work.[48] Real wages increased, and living standards considerably improved as people abandoned subsistence-level agriculture en masse.[49] Without immigration, industrialization would have slowed, as was seen in the oppressive atmosphere of the antebellum (and later Jim Crow) American South, delaying the penetration of consumer goods and keeping living standards low.[50] Southerners like Sen. John Calhoun of South Carolina recognized their population problem and even invented bizarre theories to absolve slavery and blame the North for its inability to attract immigrants (such as that the North conspired to depopulate the South with tariffs and limits on slavery).[51]

In short, immigrants made the United States a more powerful and influential country. The fact that nearly all immigrants settled in the North likely allowed the Union to prevail in the Civil War. Immigrants made up about a quarter of Union soldiers, compared with less than

5 percent in the South, and immigrant-led manufacturing in northern cities provided the North with a critical technological advantage in the war.[52] By the 1930s, these same demographic and economic factors had set the stage for America to emerge as the world's preeminent power. Winning both world wars would have been impossible without the immigrants and their descendants from the age of unrestricted legal immigration.

Americans Repeatedly Rejected Immigration Restrictions

"But it's different now," claim immigration opponents. Is it? Throughout the free immigration period, immigration opponents made all the same arguments we still hear today. Those arguments were rejected then, and they are no more credible now.

Free immigration was championed from the beginning. George Washington's administration articulated the policy that remained essentially unchanged for a century. Alexander Hamilton's famous 1791 "Report on Manufactures" argued "it is the interest of the United States to open every possible [avenue to] emigration from abroad" because immigration was "an important resource, not only for extending the population, and with it the useful and productive labour of the country, but likewise for the prosecution of manufactures."[53]

Given these views, it was no surprise that the first federal statute relating to noncitizens, the Naturalization Act of 1790, did not adopt *any* restrictions on immigration.[54] While most nations had no permanent naturalization laws at all, the Naturalization Act of 1790 was the most liberal naturalization law in the world at the time, having no partisan, religious, language, skills, or national origin requirements for immigrants to become US citizens.[55] Though it unfairly prohibited nonwhite immigrants from naturalizing, their descendants would receive citizenship by birth.[56] Moreover, nothing in the statute—or any other statute—limited anyone of any race, religion, language, or country from around the world from establishing legal residence in the United States. Proponents of this openness argued that "every person, rich or poor, must add to our wealth and strength, in a greater or less degree" (Rep. Joseph Lawrence of Pennsylvania), and they criticized the idea of establishing a deportation policy to "banish the unworthy" as akin to an "inquisition" (Rep. John Page of Virginia).[57]

Americans also rejected the first deportation statute. A decade after the American Founding, Congress briefly adopted a deportation statute for the first time: the Alien Friends Act, which empowered the president to deport individual immigrants (from "friendly" nations not at war with the United States) if he suspected they were "treasonous."[58] James Madison and Thomas Jefferson asserted that the Alien Friends Act was unconstitutional because it short-circuited the due process required by the Constitution. Madison argued that deportation was "the severest of punishments" and should only be imposed after the due process required by the Constitution. "If aliens had no rights under the constitution," he wrote, "they might not only be banished, but even capitally punished, without a jury or the other incidents to a fair trial."[59]

Meanwhile, Jefferson questioned why anyone would more trust the "bare suspicions of the President, than the solid right of innocence," which allowed him to deliver perhaps the most famous description of the purpose of the US Constitution: "let no more be heard of confidence in man, but bind him down from mischief by the chains of the Constitution." Jefferson concluded: "the friendless alien has been selected as the safest subject of a first experiment [with tyranny]; but the citizen will soon follow."[60] Jefferson and Madison won the argument, and President John Adams and the other Federalists were swept out of power in the elections of 1800, and the Alien Friends Act went out with them.[61] But the Alien Friends Act debate was less about nativism and more about the limits of presidential power to remove specific alleged threats, not to close the borders in general.[62] Proponents like Adams emphasized in that debate that they still favored "making our country an asylum for virtue in distress."[63]

The first significant anti-immigrant movement did not appear until the 1840s. Colloquially known as the Know Nothings, the American Party was founded in response to rising Catholic immigration, primarily from Ireland. But it failed to achieve its goals. In the 1860 election, the Know Nothings were replaced as a prominent national party by Republicans led by presidential candidate Abraham Lincoln. Lincoln loathed the party, writing, "When the Know-Nothings get control, [the

Declaration of Independence] will read 'all men are created equal, except negroes, and foreigners, and Catholics.' . . . When it comes to this, I should prefer emigrating to some country where they make no pretence of loving liberty."[64] Lincoln argued that immigrants could become Americans. They had, Lincoln wrote, "a right to claim [the founding] as though they were blood of the blood, and flesh of the flesh of the men who wrote that Declaration."[65]

Given Lincoln's attitude, the Republican Party platform promised to encourage immigration:

> [F]oreign immigration, which in the past has added so much to the wealth, development of resources and increase of power to the nation, the asylum of the oppressed of all nations, should be fostered and encouraged by a liberal and just policy.[66]

The encouragement of immigration was accomplished by the Immigration Act of 1864, which allowed businesses to contract with immigrants abroad and pay to bring them to the United States.[67] In addition, the Burlingame–Seward Treaty of 1868, which intended to establish trade and good relations with the Qing Dynasty, explicitly affirmed the right of "free migration" for Chinese nationals to the United States.[68]

In 1866, Congress adopted the Fourteenth Amendment to the Constitution, which codified birthright citizenship. The amendment, which has guaranteed citizenship and equal rights to all people born in the United States, even applied to the only deportable noncitizens at the time, illegally trafficked slaves.[69] Moreover, the ratifiers rejected objections that the amendment would entitle children of all immigrants from every country to US citizenship, even if their parents were ineligible to naturalize themselves.[70] Opponents denounced granting citizenship to the children of certain immigrants, whom they called "invaders" and "trespassers" like the Chinese and "Gypsies."[71] Proponents mocked the whole idea of an immigrant invasion.[72] "The only invasion of Pennsylvania within my recollection was an invasion . . . of rebels," retorted Sen. John Conness of California.[73]

By the end of the 19th century, free immigration was widely seen as a fundamental American tradition. When President Rutherford B. Hayes vetoed the first Chinese Exclusion Act in 1879, which was pitched as a special exception to the general rule, he spoke of the "*American* doctrines of free migration to and fro among the peoples and races of the earth."[74] When President Woodrow Wilson vetoed a bill in 1915 that would have required all immigrants to pass a "literacy test," he said it would "reverse the policy of all the generations of Americans that have gone before" because it would "close entirely the gates of asylum which have always been open."[75]

This bipartisan rejection of restrictions largely continued until 1917. Presidents of both parties vetoed legislation in 1897, 1913, and 1915 that included literacy tests to require all adult immigrants to be able to read.[76] In 1897, President Grover Cleveland called a literacy test a "radical departure from our national policy."[77] He said, "A century's stupendous growth, largely due to the assimilation and thrift of millions of sturdy and patriotic adopted citizens, attests the success of this generous and free-handed policy" of the Founders. Cleveland systematically dismantled each excuse justifying restriction, noting that economic downturns, not immigration, caused unemployment. During the free immigration era, unemployment's "natural consequences must be to check the further immigration," leaving no need for government intervention.[78] He concluded that the literacy test was just "the pretext for exclusion" rather than based on any serious objection to the economic or social effects of immigrants who could not read.

The Baseless Origins of Immigration Restrictions

With the astounding economic success of unrestricted immigration and the strong American tradition in favor of it, the push for immigration restrictions was fueled primarily by bigotry against specific nationalities.

Restriction was the triumph of politics over sound policy. The Page Act of 1875, barring Chinese "prostitutes" (in effect, all Chinese women), and the Chinese Exclusion Act of 1882, barring all Chinese "laborers," were the first significant immigration restrictions in American history.[79] One reason restrictionism had failed in earlier times in American history was that, although movements often appeared at a state level, they could never build a national consensus. However, Chinese exclusion broke that model. Despite its narrow regional interest, the Democrats and Republicans were competing for California's toss-up electoral votes in the extremely close presidential elections of 1876 and 1880.[80] Since Chinese immigrants were barred from naturalization by the courts because they were not "white" enough for the Naturalization Act, and they had few US-born children, neither party courted Chinese immigrants living in California, and both advocated for restriction.[81]

Calls for restricting immigration were premised on racial tropes, not economic necessity. Although advocates layered on a thin coating of labor protectionism, it was clear that most Chinese immigrants were competing with other European immigrants and were being singled out based on their race, not for economic reasons. Sen. John Miller of California—author of the Chinese Exclusion Act—argued that a vote against exclusion would be "a shout of welcome across the Pacific to the myriad hosts of the strange people," labeling the Chinese an "alien and servile race" and a "non-assimilative, heterogeneous people, utterly unfit for and incapable of self-government."[82] The response in a letter from Chinese immigrants in San Francisco—that they were "peaceful and industrious"—was ignored.[83]

In the late 19th and early 20th centuries, race eugenics—the "improvement" of the population through selective breeding—became the primary justification for broader immigration restrictions.[84] Immigrants grew less politically popular after immigration flows shifted toward Eastern Europe. In 1907, restrictionists in Congress—who had repeatedly lost the argument—created a commission to supposedly investigate immigration, chaired by anti-immigrant Sen. William Dillingham of Vermont and stacked with other restrictionists. Despite the explicit intent to use its reports to justify restriction, the Dillingham Commission found immigrants were, on average, no more likely to commit crimes[85] and no more taxing on the government or charitable organizations than the US-born.[86] Instead, the Dillingham Commission appealed to phony race "science," absurdly claiming that 67 percent of Polish Jewish immigrant students and 64 percent of southern Italian immigrant students were "retarded" and genetically inferior because they were behind in school compared with their peers.[87] This bias led the commission to conclude that, although immigrants in general were not a problem in most areas, southern and eastern Europeans supposedly were.

The Dillingham Commission published its report in 1911, recommending the literacy test for entry, but it took World War I to prompt Congress to pass any new laws. Congress finally passed the literacy test along with a total ban on Asian immigration into law over President Wilson's veto in the Immigration Act of 1917.[88] The literacy test's author and lead sponsor from 1890 onward, Sen. Henry Cabot Lodge from Massachusetts, articulated the eugenicist fears motivating the bill: "If a lower race mixes with a higher in sufficient numbers, history teaches us that the lower race will prevail."[89] Literacy rates in eastern Europe were low in the 1890s when Lodge first proposed the law, so his test would keep out people he considered to belong to "lower races."

However, by the 1920s, literacy had spread, so after the law's passage, relatively few immigrants were excluded, and race eugenicists pivoted to advocating for overt race-based numerical limits on immigration. Congressman Albert Johnson of Washington, the author of the temporary Emergency Quota of 1921 and the Immigration Act of 1924, was also president of the Eugenics Research Association, an organization that promoted immigration caps, forced sterilization, and prohibitions on interracial marriage.[90] The 1924 law, which imposed the first caps on European immigration, also preserved bans on all Asian immigration, saving the lowest limits for immigrants from Africa, the Middle East, and eastern and southern Europe.[91] Meanwhile, it granted much higher limits to western Europeans, well beyond the demand from those countries at the time. The purpose was to exclude "undesirable races" without explicitly using racial terms.[92]

President Calvin Coolidge, who signed the law, justified the extreme restriction by claiming that "biological laws tell us that certain divergent people will not mix or blend."[93] Opponents of the law, including Rep. Peter Francis Tague of Boston, mocked the crude racist arguments, noting that "the pseudo scientific claims of the sponsors of the bill" were not "substantiated from any scientific source."[94] Nonetheless, Congressman Johnson called the 1924 Act "America's second declaration of independence," but one grounded in an opposite principle: the inequality of people.[95] He proclaimed, "The day of unalloyed welcome to all peoples, the day of indiscriminate acceptance of all races, has definitely ended."[96] Adolf Hitler took notice and praised the United

States as the "one state in which one can observe at least weak beginnings of a better conception" of citizenship.[97] The law would later prevent many European Jews from escaping the Nazis in the 1930s and 1940s, as visa denials and waiting lists exploded.[98]

The Immigration Act of 1924 accomplished its goal of dramatically lowering legal immigration, but illegal immigration grew in response. At that time, no one was confused by the origin of "illegal" immigration. Nearly everyone in America knew the new prohibition had created it, and people referred to the phenomenon as "bootlegging in humans," a nod to Prohibition, which was then in effect. That was a fitting comparison, since Prohibition had proven no more effective at keeping people from acquiring alcoholic beverages than immigration restrictions would prove in keeping people from illegally crossing the border. "While legal immigration has been curbed to the extent that advocates of the new policy expected, that of the illegal—the 'bootlegging'—kind has probably increased greatly," the *New York Times* reported in 1925. "Some officials estimate that immigrants have been coming in clandestinely at a rate of at least 100 a day."[99]

Congress had already had decades of experience with illegal entries to evade the Chinese Exclusion Act, so it knew the new law would create illegal immigration, necessitating the simultaneous creation of the Border Patrol.[100] Over the next century, Border Patrol agents would make nearly 60 million arrests, struggling and failing to enforce the legal immigration prohibition.[101]

Immigration Restrictions Have Prevented Most Legal Immigration for over a Century

Although the Immigration Act of 1924 has been modified at various times, the fundamental framework of placing a cap on immigration and giving preferences to certain family members of US citizens remains the basic framework of America's legal immigration system. Before the immigration acts in the 1920s, people were presumed eligible to immigrate to the United States, and the government had to prove that they fell into an ineligible category, such as being a criminal. Since 1924, the presumption has flipped. Now, all immigrants are presumed ineligible *unless* they prove they fall into an exception. Before

Figure 2

Immigrants are being approved for permanent residence at an all–time low rate

Share of immigrants approved for legal permanent residence, FY 1883–2024

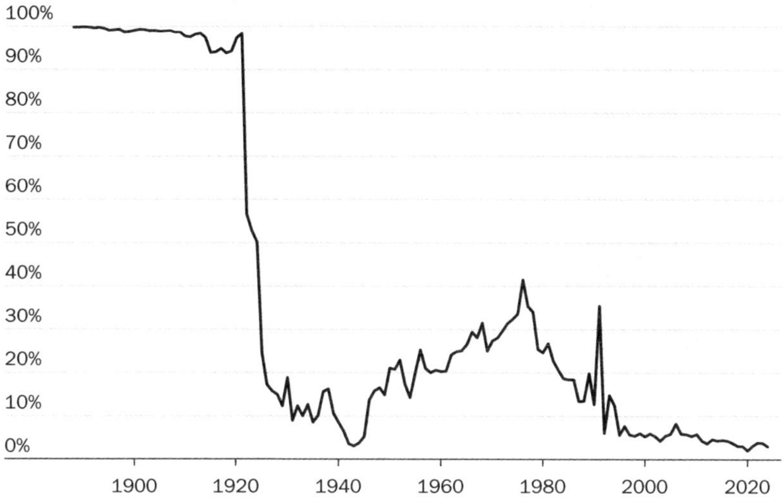

Source: David J. Bier, "Green Card Approval Rate Reaches Record Lows," Cato Institute Briefing Paper No. 173, February 15, 2024.

the 1920s, 98 percent of all legal immigrant applicants were approved. Today, the share is just 3 percent (Figure 2).[102]

Many people believe that the Founders' vision is no longer relevant in today's America. Some say that the vision of America as an asylum is antiquated when most immigrants today come mainly for economic reasons, but the same has been true at every moment of American history,[103] and the Founders saw economic conditions as a reflection of the tyranny that immigrants faced at home.[104] Some say a greater economic need existed at the Founding, but the opposite is true. Near-subsistence level farming, which was the work of the overwhelming majority of Americans at the time, contributes almost nothing economically to the rest of society. Most population growth came from natural reproduction, as Jefferson and others noted at the time, while the natural-born working-age population is already shrinking today.[105] Some say that the fiscal burden on the government is too large today, but the fiscal benefit from immigrants has never been greater.[106]

Some say immigrants are less skilled today, but they have never been more skilled or economically productive.[107] Some say immigrants and their children will not learn English, but they are even more likely to learn English than those in the early 20th century.[108] Some say immigrants come from countries where they will never accept our system of government, but immigrants today are far more likely to come from democracies than ever before—or to long for democracy if they are escaping dictatorships.[109] Some say immigrants today are more prone to crime, but in fact, they are not only underrepresented in prisons compared with the US-born, but also compared with immigrants of the early 20th century.[110] Some say reforming legal immigration is impossible so long as illegal immigration persists, but it is precisely because legal immigration is impossible for them that so many immigrants come illegally.[111]

The single most important fact about the history of immigration policy in the United States is that free immigration ended not because the system was failing to produce positive results for the country or because economic and social realities changed, but because politicians accepted phony racist science and exploited prejudice against new immigrants. Restrictionists used every argument they could, just as they do today, but the centrality of racism was widely acknowledged (and even celebrated) at the time. Free immigration did not end because of any purported problems. It ended because opponents rejected the Founders' vision and claimed that those immigrants could never become true Americans. They were wrong then. Their intellectual heirs are wrong now.

Notes

1. George Washington to Joshua Holmes, December 2, 1783, Papers of George Washington, Founders Online, National Archives.

2. George Washington to Francis Adrian Vanderkemp, May 28, 1788, Teaching American History.

3. Thomas Paine, *Common Sense* (Philadelphia, 1776).

4. Samuel Adams, "On American Independence (1776)," in *The World's Famous Orations*, vol. 8, ed. William J. Bryan (Funk and Wagnalls, 1906).

5. John Locke, "Two Treatises of Government" (London, 1690; Project Gutenberg, 2003), secs. 118, 122.

6. Thomas Jefferson, "Thomas Jefferson, A Summary View of the Rights of British America," July 1774.

7. Thomas Jefferson to Jean Nicolas Démeunier, April 29, 1795, in *The Papers of Thomas Jefferson*, vol. 28, *January 1, 1794–February 29, 1796*, ed. John Catanzariti (Princeton University Press, 2000), pp. 340–42.

8. "Declaration of Independence," a transcription, America's Founding Documents, National Archives.

9. John Adams to James Warren, March 21, 1783, Papers of John Adams, vol. 14, Massachusetts Historical Society.

10. "Madison Debates," August 9, 1787, The Avalon Project, Yale Law School Lillian Goldman Law Library.

11. David J. Bier, "The Founding Fathers Favored a Liberal Immigration System," *Cato at Liberty* (blog), March 27, 2018.

12. "Madison Debates," August 10, 1787.

13. Alexander Hamilton, "Report on Manufactures," December 5, 1791 (William Brown, 1827).

14. George Washington to Joshua Holmes, December 2, 1783.

15. Thomas Jefferson, *Autobiography with the Declaration of Independence*, The Avalon Project, Yale Law School Lillian Goldman Law Library, January 6, 1821.

16. James H. Hutson, "The Founding Fathers and Islam: Library Papers Show Early Tolerance for Muslim Faith," *Library of Congress Information Bulletin* 61, no. 5 (May 2002).

17. Benjamin Franklin, *The Autobiography of Benjamin Franklin*, chap. 10, Varsity Tutors.

18. George Washington to the Hebrew Congregation in Newport, Rhode Island, August 18, 1790, in *The Papers of George Washington*, Presidential Series, vol. 6, *1 July 1790–30 November 1790*, ed. Mark A. Mastromarino (University Press of Virginia, 1996), pp. 284–86 (emphasis added).

19. James Madison, *Federalist* no. 10, November 22, 1787, Founders Online, National Archives.

20. Bier, "The Founding Fathers Favored a Liberal Immigration System."

21. Gaillard Hunt, ed., *The Writings of James Madison, Comprising His Public Papers and His Private Correspondence*, vol. 4 (1787) (G. P. Putnam's Sons, 1900).

22. Janakee Chavda, "Immigrants and Children of Immigrants Make up at Least 15% of 119th Congress," Pew Research Center, February 27, 2025.

23. Aristide R. Zolberg, *A Nation by Design: Immigration Policy in the Fashioning of America* (Harvard University Press, 2008).

24. Alexander Hamilton, "*Alexander Hamilton's Final Version of the Report on the Subject of Manufactures*," December 5, 1791, in *The Papers of Alexander Hamilton*, vol. 10, *December 1791–January 1792*, ed. Harold C. Syrett (Columbia University Press, 1966), pp. 230–340.

25. George Washington to John Adams, November 15, 1794, in *The Papers of George Washington*, Presidential Series, vol. 17, *October 1, 1794–March 31, 1795*, ed. David R. Hoth and Carol S. Ebel (University of Virginia Press, 2013), pp. 161–62.

26. Benjamin Franklin, "Observations Concerning the Increase of Mankind, 1751," in *The Papers of Benjamin Franklin*, vol. 4, *July 1, 1750, through June 30, 1753*, ed. Leonard W. Labaree (Yale University Press, 1961), pp. 225–34.

27. Benjamin Franklin to Peter Collinson, May 9, 1753, Teaching American History.

28. "Benjamin Franklin on Immigration," in Benjamin Franklin, *The Papers of Benjamin Franklin*, vol. 42 (Yale University Press, 2017). Franklin similarly reversed his opinion about Africans in America: Benjamin Franklin to John Adams, February 9, 1790, in John Adams, *The Adams Papers*, vol. 20, *June 1789–February 1791*, ed. Sara Georgini et al. (Harvard University Press, 2020), pp. 236–38.

29. John Quincy Adams would reiterate these comments in 1819: "Emigration to the U. States," *Niles' Weekly Register*, June 4, 1819.

30. Thomas Jefferson, "Resolutions Relative to the Alien and Sedition Acts," November 10, 1798, in *The Writings of Thomas Jefferson*, vol. 1, ed. Andrew A. Lipscomb and Albert Ellery Bergh (Thomas Jefferson Memorial Association, 1905).

31. In particular, Alexander Hamilton, "The Examination Number VII," January 7, 1802, in *The Papers of Alexander Hamilton*, vol. 25, *July 1800–April 1802*, ed. Harold C. Syrett (Columbia University Press, 1977), pp. 491–95.

32. Thomas Jefferson, "Overturning Federalist Alien Acts," 1802, *Monticello.org.*

33. Helen Doe, *The First Atlantic Liner: Brunel's Great Western Steamship* (Amberley, 2017).

34. David J. Bier, "Immigrant Population Is Still One Million Below the Pre-Trump Trend," *Cato at Liberty* (blog), September 13, 2024; and Campbell Gibson and Kay Jung, "Historical Census Statistics on the Foreign-Born Population of the United States: 1850 to 2000," Population Division Working Paper no. 81, US Census Bureau, February 2006.

35. "Yearbook of Immigration Statistics," Office of Homeland Security Statistics, Department of Homeland Security, last updated February 11, 2025.

36. Gibson and Jung, "Historical Census Statistics on the Foreign-Born Population of the United States: 1850 to 2000."

37. Gibson and Jung, "Historical Census Statistics on the Foreign-Born Population of the United States: 1850 to 2000."

38. Matt Stirn, "What Archaeologists Are Learning About the Lives of the Chinese Immigrants Who Built the Transcontinental Railroad," *Smithsonian Magazine*, April 2022.

39. Richard White, *Railroaded: The Transcontinentals and the Making of Modern America* (W. W. Norton and Company, 2011).

40. Gail Gamache et al., *West Meets East: Americans Adopt Chinese Children* (Bergin & Garvey, 1999).

41. Charles Hirschman and Elizabeth Mogford, "Immigration and the American Industrial Revolution from 1880 to 1920," *Social Science Research* 38, no. 4 (December 2009): 897–920.

42. Georgios P. Loizides and Subhash R. Sonnad, "Fordist Applied Research in the Era of the Five-Dollar Day," Peer Reviewed Article 10 (Sociology Department, Grand Valley State University, Fall 2004).

43. Hirschman and Mogford, "Immigration and the American Industrial Revolution from 1880 to 1920."

44. "Yearbook of Immigration Statistics, 2024."

45. Richard H. Steckel, "A History of the Standard of Living in the United States," EH.Net Encyclopedia, ed. Robert Whaples, July 21, 2002.

46. "Maddison Project Database 2023," Groningen Growth and Development Centre, 2024; and Jutta Bolt and Jan Luiten van Zanden, "Maddison-Style

Estimates of the Evolution of the World Economy: A New 2023 Update," *Journal of Economic Surveys* 39, no. 2 (2025): 631–71.

47. "Italian Immigration," Digital History, 2021; David E. Nye, *Electrifying America: Social Meanings of a New Technology, 1880-1940* (MIT Press, 1992); and Lily Rothman, "How Immigration Helped the United States Get Its First Subway System," *TIME*, January 31, 2017.

48. Richard Sutch, "Hard Work, Nonemployment, and the Wealth-Age Profile: Evidence of a Life-Cycle Strategy in the United States During the Nineteenth Century," National Bureau of Economic Research Development of the American Economy, Program Meeting, Cambridge, Massachusetts, February 17, 2011.

49. "Bicentennial Edition: Historical Statistics of the United States, Colonial Times to 1970," US Census Bureau, September 1975; and Steven Mintz, "Statistics: Trends in American Farming," The Gilder Lehrman Institute of American History.

50. "The South was not linked to this international system [of labor], but it should be clear by now that the explanation lies in the realm of social institutions and social choice rather than in sheer barriers of distance and cost." Gavin Wright, *Old South, New South: Revolutions in the Southern Economy Since the Civil War* (Basic Books, 1986), p. 74.

51. John C. Calhoun, *The Works of John C. Calhoun*, vol. 4 (Jazzybee Verlag, n.d.), p. 303.

52. Harold Holzer, *Brought Forth on This Continent: Abraham Lincoln and American Immigration* (Penguin, 2024), pp. 186, 204, 414.

53. Hamilton, "Alexander Hamilton's Final Version of the Report on the Subject of Manufactures."

54. Naturalization Act of 1790, 1st Cong., 1st sess., 1790.

55. Zolberg, *A Nation by Design*; and Andrew M. Baxter and Alex Nowrasteh, "A Brief History of U.S. Immigration Policy from the Colonial Period to the Present Day," Cato Institute Policy Analysis no. 919, August 3, 2021.

56. Except from 1857 to 1868, between the *Dred Scott* decision and the ratification of the Fourteenth Amendment. See: "*Dred Scott v Sandford*: The Dissents," 1856, Famous Trials: Accounts and Materials for 100 of History's Most Important Trials, UMKC School of Law; and William Rawle, A *View of the Constitution of the United States of America* (P. H. Nicklin, 1829), p. 86.

57. *Annals of Congress*, "Rule of Naturalization," February 3, 1790, vol. 1, pp. 1153–54, Congress.gov.

58. "An Act Concerning Aliens," 5th Cong., 2nd sess., chap. 58, June 25, 1798.

59. Andy Craig, "Does the Constitution Give the Federal Government the Power to Banish Foreigners?," James Madison on the Unconstitutionality of Immigration, Libertarianism.org, October 1, 2021.

60. Jefferson, "Resolutions Relative to the Alien and Sedition Acts."

61. The Alien Enemies Act, on the other hand, persisted, but it could be used only during a war. In the War of 1812, it was invoked to require registration and relocation of unnaturalized British immigrants to 40 miles inland, if designed by a US Marshal. Even then, immigrants could receive review of those relocation orders in US courts. See Adam Klein and Benjamin Wittes, "Preventive Detention in American Theory and Practice," *Harvard National Security Journal* 2, no. 1 (2011): 85–191.

62. Only Alexander Hamilton, reversing his former position on immigration, appeared to adopt this interpretation: Hamilton, "The Examination Number VII."

63. John Adams, *The Works of John Adams, Second President of the United States: with a Life of the Author, Notes and Illustrations*, vol. 9, *Letters and State Papers 1799–1811*, ed. Charles Francis Adams (Little, Brown and Co., 1856), p. 275.

64. Abraham Lincoln to Joshua Speed, August 24, 1855, Abraham Lincoln Online.

65. Abraham Lincoln, "Electric Cord Speech," Chicago, Illinois, July 10, 1858, in Lincoln, *The Collected Works of Abraham Lincoln*, vol. 2, ed. Roy P. Basler (Rutgers University Press, 1953), pp. 499–500.

66. "Republican Party Platform of 1864," The American Presidency Project, UC Santa Barbara, June 7, 1864.

67. Immigration Act of 1864, 38th Cong., 1st sess., 1864.

68. "Burlingame–Seward Treaty (1868)," Wikisource, last edited February 18, 2025.

69. Gabriel J. Chin and Paul Finkelman, "Birthright Citizenship, Slave Trade Legislation, and the Origins of Federal Immigration Regulation," *University of California Davis Law Review* 54 (2021): 2215–65.

70. James C. Ho, "Defining 'American': Birthright Citizenship and the Original Understanding of the 14th Amendment," *The Green Bag* 9, no. 4 (Summer 2006): 367–78.

71. *Congressional Globe*, May 30, 1866, p. 2891.

72. *Congressional Globe*, May 30, 1866, p. 2892.

73. *Congressional Globe*, May 30, 1866, p. 2892.

74. Rutherford B. Hayes, "Veto Message Regarding Immigration Legislation," University of Virginia, Miller Center, March 1, 1879 (emphasis added).

75. Woodrow Wilson, "Veto of Immigration Legislation," University of Virginia, Miller Center, January 28, 1915.

76. Grover Cleveland, "Veto Message Regarding Immigration Legislation," University of Virginia, Miller Center, March 2, 1897; William Howard Taft, "Message to the Senate Returning Without Approval 'An Act to Regulate the Immigration of Aliens to and the Residence of Aliens in the United States,'" The American Presidency Project, UC Santa Barbara, February 14, 1913; and Wilson, "Veto of Immigration Legislation."

77. Cleveland, "Veto Message Regarding Immigration Legislation."

78. Cleveland, "Veto Message Regarding Immigration Legislation."

79. Page Act of 1875, 43rd Cong., 2nd sess., chap. 141; "Ulysses S. Grant, Chinese Immigration, and the Page Act of 1875," National Park Service, last updated November 22, 2021; and Chinese Exclusion Act of 1882, 47th Cong., 1st sess., chap. 117–20, 126, May 6, 1882.

80. Andrew Gyory, *Closing the Gate: Race, Politics, and the Chinese Exclusion Act* (University of North Carolina Press, 1998).

81. Case No. 104: In Re Ah Yup, Circuit Court, D. California, April 29, 1878.

82. "Miller's Speech; Synopsis of an Earnest Appeal to Congress," TeachUSHistory.org, February 28, 1882.

83. Otis Gibson, *The Chinese in America* (Hitchcock & Walden, 1877), p. 289.

84. Daniel Okrent, *The Guarded Gate: Bigotry, Eugenics and the Law That Kept Two Generations of Jews, Italians, and Other Europeans Out of America* (Scribner, 2019).

85. William Paul Dillingham, *Abstract of the Report on Immigration and Crime* (Government Printing Office, 1911).

86. William Paul Dillingham, *Immigrants as Charity Seekers* (Government Printing Office, 1911).

87. John M. Lund, "Boundaries of Restriction: The Dillingham Commission," *University of Vermont History Review* 6 (December 1994).

88. Immigration Act of 1917, 64th Cong., 2nd sess., H.R. 10384, ch. 29, February 5, 1917.

89. Henry Cabot Lodge, *Speeches and Addresses, 1884–1909* (Houghton Mifflin, 1909), p. 264.

90. Paul R. D. Lawrie, *Forging a Laboring Race: The African American Worker in the Progressive Imagination* (NYU Press, 2016).

91. Immigration Act of 1924, 68th Cong., 1st sess., ch. 190 H.R. 7996, May 26, 1924.

92. Alex Nowrasteh, "Reflections on the Immigration Act of 1924," *Cato at Liberty* (blog), June 1, 2016.

93. Daniel Okrent, "A Century Ago, America Built Another Kind of Wall," *New York Times*, May 3, 2019.

94. 68 Cong. Rec. H5833 (April 8, 1924).

95. "Statement of Albert Johnson," National Affairs, *Time*, April 28, 1924.

96. Roy Lawrence Garis, *Immigration Restriction: A Study of the Opposition to and Regulation of Immigration into the United States* (Macmillan, 1927).

97. James Q. Whitman, *Hitler's American Model: The United States and the Making of Nazi Race Law* (Princeton University Press, 2017), p. 46.

98. David J. Bier, "Green Card Approval Rate Reaches Record Lows," Cato Institute Briefing Paper no. 173, February 15, 2024.

99. David Bier, "Tougher Restrictions on Immigrants Won't Work," *Newsweek*, November 21, 2016.

100. Erika Lee, *At America's Gates: Chinese Immigration During the Exclusion Era, 1882–1943* (University of North Carolina Press, 2004); and "Border Patrol History," US Customs and Border Protection, October 22, 2020.

101. "United States Border Patrol: Nationwide Encounters Fiscal Years 1925–2020," US Customs and Border Protection.

102. Bier, "Green Card Approval Rate Reaches Record Lows."

103. Timothy J. Hatton and Jeffrey G. Williamson, *The Age of Mass Migration: Causes and Economic Impact* (Oxford University Press, 1998).

104. See, for instance, Tench Coxe: "Emigration from Europe will also relieve and assist us. The blessings of civil and religious liberty in America and the oppressions of most foreign governments, the want of employment at home and the expectations of profit here, curiosity, domestic unhappiness, civil wars, and various other circumstances will bring many manufacturers to this asylum for mankind." See: Tench Coxe, "Job Creation," *Lapham's Quarterly*, 1787; Hamilton, "Report on Manufactures."

105. As Jefferson, Monroe, and others noted at the time.

106. David J. Bier, "A Century of Immigrants Improving Government Budgets," Cato Institute Policy Analysis, forthcoming.

107. Jens Manuel Krogstad and Jynnah Radford, "Education Levels of U.S. Immigrants are on the Rise," Pew Research, Short Reads, September 14, 2018.

108. Ran Abramitzky and Leah Boustan, *Streets of Gold: America's Untold Story of Immigrant Success* (PublicAffairs, 2022), p. 113.

109. David J. Bier, "More Immigrants Come From Democracies Today Than Prior Waves," *Cato at Liberty* (blog), Cato Institute, May 3, 2018.

110. Ran Abramitzky et al., "Law-Abiding Immigrants: The Incarceration Gap Between Immigrants and the US-Born, 1870–2020," *American Economic Review: Insights* 6, no. 4 (December 2024): 453–71.

111. David J. Bier, "Why Legal Immigration Is Nearly Impossible: U.S. Legal Immigration Rules Explained," Cato Institute Policy Analysis no. 950, June 13, 2023.

6

THE WITHERING OF THE OLD REPUBLIC—THE DECLINE OF ANTI-MILITARISM IN AMERICAN POLITICS

BRANDAN P. BUCK

He has kept among us, in Times of Peace, Standing Armies without the Consent of our legislatures.

He has affected to render the Military independent of and superior to the Civil power.

If America is again to have government 'by consent of the governed,' one part must offer the alternative position. That alternative is, of course, individual freedom and private enterprise." Such was the declaration of retired Republican Rep. Howard Buffett from Nebraska in his 1962 article "An Opportunity for the Republican Party," published in the libertarian magazine *New Individualist Review*. Buffett's article centered on conscription, which had become an accepted practice by the early 1960s but was one that he maintained to be an "Old World evil." Buffett's piece lamented that conscription, along with other trappings of the Cold War state, fundamentally transformed American society, an alteration made possible by a collapsed political environment. Buffett argued that his once-beloved Republican Party, born of anti-slavery agitation, had become one of "me-tooism," having joined the Democrats in embracing the permanent wartime state. In Buffett's telling, the American Republic's plunge into imperial adventurism occurred as both parties succumbed to the machinations of technocratically managed society, first through the New Deal's welfare state, then solidified by the needs of the warfare state. His article was one last attempt to convince the GOP to take "a stand against the peacetime conscription of American youth" and thereby, once again, "become the party of freedom."[1]

Buffett's strident positions on militarism and its impact on American civil and economic life were neither partisan nor iterations of disembodied ideas inherited from the Founders. Nor was he alone in holding them; he was not an isolated gadfly. During the first half of the 20th century, American anti-militarists were a political remnant of a once-vigorous political sensibility formed during America's rise to global prominence, reaching the apex of their influence after World War I. These opponents of American militarism, in both Congress and the media, believed that the creation of a large standing army, particularly via conscription, fundamentally altered the individual's relationship to the state, while corroding civil liberties and the domestic economy. These opponents of militarism reached their height of political relevance in the wake of the First World War. But the Second World War and its related political realignments contained and eventually strangled the final voices of opposition to the increasing role of the military in society and its effect on American civil liberties.

On the eve of American entry into World War I, Southern populist Democrats and Midwestern progressive Republicans drew on an earlier understanding of America's relationship with militarism. Both factions believed, as the Founders once held, that creating a large standing army would fundamentally alter the nature of the American Republic. Congressional opposition to a large army was especially strident regarding conscription. Congressional opponents of the draft to support American entry into World War I believed that, if enacted, it would transform American society into a replica of what it was mobilizing to fight: a martial society. Democratic Rep. Charles H. Brand of Georgia remarked that the conscription bill, as proposed, exempted government officers. According to Brand, these officials would enjoy the fruits of "life, liberty, and freedom" while deciding "who shall go to war and who shall remain at home."[2]

Brand's fellow conscription opponents echoed these sentiments. One was Republican Rep. Ernest Lundeen (MN), who opposed conscription as fervently as he did American entry into the war. Like Brand, Lundeen asserted that the draft was undemocratic, as it left Congress untouched. According to Lundeen, this disparity in sacrifice undermined the lofty ideals for which the United States was to enter the war and eroded the difference between America and its Old-World adversaries. The fear of a disfigured republic was bipartisan. Summing up this bipartisan opposition to American entry into World War I and its ramifications on the home front, Democratic Missouri Sen. William J. Stone stated, "I won't vote for this war because if we go into it, we will never again have the same old Republic."[3]

Anti-war efforts in Congress were supported by a cadre of liberal and progressive journalists, such as Oswald Garrison Villard. Writing in the *New York Evening Post* in an article aptly titled "Preparedness Is Militarism," Villard lauded congressional opposition and asserted that by preparing for war overseas, the United States was undermining its unique republican character. Villard argued that military preparedness signified "an entire change in our attitude towards the military," one that eschewed the nation's traditional "suspicion and distrust" of large military establishment inherited from the Founding Fathers.[4]

While these dissidents could not stop America's entry into the war, their perspective helped shape American attitudes toward militarism and its impact on civil liberties as the nation returned to peacetime. Wartime civil liberties abuses stemming from the Sedition Act of 1918, Woodrow Wilson's proposals to corporatize the economy, and postwar revelations of American and British propaganda shocked Americans—and, for prewar anti-militarists, served as evidence for their arguments.[5] On civil liberties and the right of free speech, Villard asserted that the newspapers had transformed into agents of the state, essential cogs of its war machine. In a speech to the Illinois Press Association, Villard charged, "Every newspaper man now knows . . . that we of the profession were merely agents of government propaganda . . . during the World War."[6] *The Freeman*, a progressive magazine, called the federal government's domestic propaganda campaign "a poison gas attack."[7] From his perch at *The Saturday Evening Post*, columnist Garet Garrett called the propaganda threat "so new and so bewildering that not only has no solution for it been imagined but it has not been adequately defined."[8]

On the material issues associated with militarism, prewar anti-militarists found the interwar period amenable to their views. Chastened by the First World War, once-hawkish Northern political figures, industrialists, and naval power enthusiasts backed efforts to disarm, having come around to the idea that American export markets could better achieve the goals of American diplomacy.[9] Outside elite circles, fear of the corrosive power of large standing armies and militarized economies became a common feature of American popular culture. The American zeitgeist during the interwar period yielded works of social commentary like the *New York Times* bestseller *Merchants of Death*, coauthored by progressive H. C. Engelbrecht and conservative Frank Hanighen, as well as a national enthusiasm for investigative journalism that reinforced popular attitudes and solidified noninterventionist politics on Capitol Hill.[10]

Total War in the Old Republic

The Second World War and the New Deal's reordering of the American economy cracked this once-dominant perspective. Political opposition to a large standing army withered as America's sectional politics shifted during President Franklin Delano Roosevelt's administration. While large pockets of the American South harbored deeply anti-militarist sentiments on the eve of World War I, such was not the case in the waning days of American neutrality during World War II. Significant electoral turnover after World War I, combined with mortality and patronage associated with the New Deal, recalibrated Southern politics into supporting the then-nascent warfare state.[11] The combination of the political attrition of older dissenting voices and a new Democratic coalition loyal to the president and his New Deal program meant that, on the eve of US entry into the next world war, the Solid South became an ardent supporter of the military preparedness and the militarization of the economy.[12] While Wilson had to contend with internal dissent, FDR, despite an intraparty divide over the New Deal and a growing rupture over domestic civil rights, could count on a Democratic Party unified on military matters.[13]

As Americans debated their country's involvement in the Second World War, the arguments from opponents of mass mobilization remained largely the same, even as their political coalition narrowed. In this changed political environment, opposition to the militarization of American society and the American economy fell largely to conservative Midwestern Republicans, who—echoing their progressive forbearers—argued that the creation of a large standing military would fundamentally alter domestic life and create the material conditions for America's entry into the war. On the eve of America's entry into World War II, these opponents of American militarism sought to derail conscription, seeing the practice as akin to slavery and the first step to a fundamental reordering of American society. Then-rising Republican conservative star Sen. Robert A. Taft of Ohio also made these arguments. In a September 1940 radio address, he argued that the draft was immoral, especially in peacetime, as it plucked individuals out of their chosen professions and livelihoods, thus harming their means of self-betterment. Therefore, he argued, conscription was "absolutely opposed to the principles of individual liberty, which have always been considered a part of American democracy."[14]

These dissidents did not just argue from abstraction but invoked the painful memories of domestic excesses surrounding American involvement in the First World War. In a December 1939 piece in *Woman's Day* titled "We Who Have Sons," libertarian writer Rose Wilder Lane objected to the prospect of another military draft. Her piece was illustrated with a collage of carefree, smiling young men, with the provocative question "Will They Be Killers?" superimposed. Lane drew on the memories of American involvement in the previous world war and the accompanying suppression of domestic liberties, including the most basic—the right to live. Lane's opposition to conscription and the prospect of fighting another war in Europe was firmly intertwined with memories of the security state that arose during the prosecution of World War I. After a scathing foreword, she explicitly referenced the imprisonment of war resisters, abridgments of free speech, and the wave of "barbarities" and "mob hates" of "stupid and brutal men."[15] She argued that such excesses, including conscription, exposed Americans to the fate of people residing in Europe's warring empires. She worried that if "America goes again to war in Europe, their freedom vanishes."[16]

The nation's second plunge into a world war dramatically and irrevocably altered American society. Still, it did not extinguish all the embers of opposition to its emerging status as a global power and its accompanying martial society. The 1942 midterms, rather than serving as a referendum on prewar "isolationists," as FDR's administration had hoped, ushered in a new crop of oppositional voices, particularly in the Midwest.[17]

One of those political newcomers soon became a key oppositional figure and remained so during the early Cold War. Nebraska Rep. Howard Buffett, like other Midwestern Republicans, feared that the New Deal represented a fundamental break with traditional American attitudes toward liberty and commerce. In a 1936 letter to former President Herbert Hoover, the then-young investment banker argued that the New Deal represented a "disaster within" that threatened future generations' "chance for liberty, for freedom, and for individual reward for individual merit."[18]

Later in Congress and with the nation at war, Buffett argued that the wartime economy and mass military mobilization threatened to make the changes of the New Deal permanent and thus change the nature of the republic forever. During the height of the Second World War, in his first congressional term, Buffett criticized the US government's policy of unconditional surrender, arguing that it needlessly prolonged the war and thereby continued its toll on American lives and the nation's economic and political health. On the House floor, he argued that the longer the war continued, the longer American soldiers would continue living "abnormal and unnatural lives," and that the US government would continue to imitate the "economic methods of nazi-ism." Summing up his position, Buffett highlighted what he believed to be the trade-off at the core of mass mobilization, asserting that "no penalties against our foes will enable us to evade the consequences of our steps away from liberty."[19]

The Freezing of the Republic

Then for a fleeting moment, in the wake of the war, it seemed that the United States would return to something closer to a condition of prewar normality. In 1946, in a brief interregnum between a world at war and the onset of the Cold War, the United States slashed its defense budgets and rapidly demobilized. Congress forced deep military spending cuts and rapid demobilization to return the country to the prewar status quo. Such cuts fit a then-prevailing mood of retrenchment, a tightening of congressional voting share between the parties,[20] and President Harry Truman's belief in the necessity for a peacetime balanced budget.[21] From the end of World War II until 1947, the United States cut its military budget from $81 billion to $13 billion and reduced the number of military personnel from 12.1 million to 1.6 million.[22]

However, this interlude of normality was not to last, as worsening relations between the United States and the Soviet Union ushered in a new iteration of elevated defense budgets and the return of peacetime conscription. The crises of the early Cold War—namely, the deepening civil war in Greece, followed by the announcement of the Truman Doctrine in 1947 and then by a communist coup in Czechoslovakia and the Soviet blockade of Berlin the following year—ignited a new wave of debate in the United States on the need for military mobilization. Into this newest conflict, a fleeting body of congressional opposition marshaled the old ideas arrayed against large standing armies and their corrosive influence on civil liberties.

From 1947 to 1949, congressional debates about the emerging national security state and the creation of a permanent military establishment elicited similar arguments from congressional opponents. Writing to his constituents via an open letter, Buffett warned that the coming showdown with the Soviet Union would bring a new wave of economic hardship and incremental entry into war. "Historically all-out military strength has required cruelly oppressive taxation," Buffett warned. He added that the federal government would move to "suppress such domestic discontent" as during the nation's previous world wars and that military preparedness brought with it the incentives for war itself. "Most modern wars have been waged by rulers promising peace" he claimed and added, "when a nation has mobilized for war the politicians must maneuver it into actual war or lose their jobs."[23] Buffett was not alone—as his fellow Midwestern Republicans had been on the eve of the World Wars—and could present an oppositional force on Capitol Hill.[24]

However, the opposition camp was fatally wounded by the Cold War's first hot engagement, the Korean War.[25] War on the Korean Peninsula accelerated a transformative process within the GOP's moderate Northern section that had begun during the Second World War, with former interventionists like Republican Sen. Arthur Vandenberg of Michigan assuming a prominent congressional role in the formation of an emerging Cold War consensus on defense spending and preparedness.[26] The Korean War helped convert several Republican stragglers, including a number of erstwhile Midwestern antimilitarists, to the militarist side. One such convert was Rep. Robert B. Chiperfield of Illinois, a moderate Republican who had posed significant opposition to increased defense spending and continuation of the draft in the wake of the Second World War. He was one of the 105 Republicans, and 136 representatives overall, who opposed the Selective Service Act in 1948 and one of 98 Republicans, and 130 representatives overall, who opposed HR 6771, the Cold War's first large military appropriation, which formed the "National Military Establishment."[27]

Despite his resistance to the early trappings of the Cold War state, Chiperfield was transformed into an ardent cold warrior during the Korean War.[28] Reminiscing in 1959, Chiperfield referred to the Second World War and the Korean War as creating "consequences" that were "grave" and "almost of a crisis nature, with which we are confronted."[29] Chiperfield's conversion was politically influential, as he sat on the House Foreign Affairs Committee, of which he had been a member since 1939. By 1953, with the onset of the Dwight D. Eisenhower administration and a GOP House majority, he became the committee chair. From his committee perch, Chiperfield was able to shape Republican Party orthodoxy on foreign affairs and did so with outsized authority informed by his conversion to interventionism.

Howard Buffett was not one of these defectors. Rather than see the Korean War as a necessitating crisis, he went as far as to blame the US government for instigating the conflict and picking a side in what amounted to a Korean civil war.[30] On the House floor and in the press, the emboldened Buffett used the Korean War to attack the underlying logic of the Cold War and its supporting policies. In a speech titled "The Evil Men in the Kremlin Must be Chortling as Militarism Runs

Wild in America," Buffett lambasted the country's growing military commitments in the wake of an escalating showdown with the Soviets. Rather than see such policies as necessary, Buffett declared that "our military expansion, with its goal of dominating the globe outside Russia's borders, will almost certainly end either in economic collapse and dictatorship in America, or global war that will lead to the same result."[31] Nor did he hide such views from his constituents. In one of his regular "Washington Report" columns, he sardonically asked a reader, "Shouldn't we give the Statue of Liberty to Canada?" He added, "Canada's young men are free. They are not being [conscripted] to die in Korea or to police Europe."[32]

Buffett was increasingly alone, however. By the 82nd Congress (1951–1953), opposition to military spending and conscription evaporated due to the death, departure, or conversion of prominent anti-war figures. Despite representing longstanding ideas within the American political consciousness, conservative Midwestern Republicans, now the lone heirs of an anti-militarist political tradition, found themselves fighting a losing battle as Democratic support for the new wartime state solidified and Republican opposition fractured along sectional lines.

Many conservative Republicans in Congress succumbed to the notion that American security required elevated defensive spending for deterrence, as they had on the eve of the Second World War. While still balking at most of the trappings of the emerging Cold War state, figures such as Herbert Hoover and Robert A. Taft came to view nuclear deterrence and, therefore, elevated defense spending as necessary for American security.[33] While these conservative Republicans advocated for a comparatively limited vision centered on hemispheric deterrence and airpower, such compromises conceded ideological ground and thereby created a consensus in Washington in favor of elevated defense spending that stood virtually unchallenged for the remainder of the Cold War. President Eisenhower's "New Look," a defense strategy centered on nuclear deterrence and formulated with cost in mind, incorporated some of the opposition's standing concerns, thereby undercutting intraparty resistance and contributing to a marked decline in Republican opposition to increased defense spending.[34]

"While I would like to throw conscription overboard . . . I can't fight this kind of battle alone, Howard."[35] Such was the response of Rep. H. R. Gross (R-IA) to his friend and former colleague Howard Buffett in March of 1963. Earlier in the month, the then-retired Buffett forwarded Gross a copy of his article in *New Individualist Review.* Despite the lack of congressional opposition, Buffett sensed an opportunity to press the issue, given the slate of upcoming bills on conscription. In forwarding his piece, Buffett asked his old friend to introduce it into the *Congressional Record*, noting that he and Gross were "fighting the battle for an honest Republican Party."[36] In a follow-up letter, Buffett praised Gross for being one of only three House members who had opposed an extension of the draft during a vote on March 11, 1963. Buffett conceded that "I know the odds you are up against" and praised his old friend for displaying "the courage of a lion."[37] Courage, however, was not enough to stem the tide of the draft and other aspects of the warfare state in the early 1960s.

In his response, Gross aired his frustrations over being a near-lone voice in opposition to conscription and other trappings of the Cold War. Gross said his efforts to delay or derail conscription using parliamentary procedure had gone "exactly nowhere."[38] He concluded that "for that reason I would prefer not to go further with this issue at this time" and noted that the contents of his letter included the returned copy of Buffett's opinion piece.

Between the end of the Korean War and the escalation of the war in Vietnam, the remaining anti-militarists in Congress either retired, as Buffett had, or, in the case of Gross, remained hopelessly outnumbered. While a smattering of congressional conservatives opposed President John F. Kennedy's ambitious "Flexible Response" defense spending program, the mass of political opinion had long settled on the need for a permanent warfare state to counter the Soviet Union.[39] As America entered the height of the Vietnam War, the remnants of political opposition to a large standing army, conscription, and other trappings of militarism had withered from the American political mainstream.

Howard Buffett died a little over a year after his correspondence with H. R. Gross. He was only 60. Buffett did not live long enough to witness the full horror of Vietnam, fed by conscription, as he had feared. He also did not live long enough to see the draft's eventual abandonment in January 1973, a movement fed in no small part by a nascent libertarian movement centered on the *New Individualist Review* and a young libertarian economist, Milton Friedman.[40] Buffett's efforts then bore fruit posthumously, though not before about 58,000 Americans, over 17,000 of them conscripts, died in the Vietnam War.

The other work of the anti-militarists like Buffett remains unfinished. As this recent history has shown, employing persuasive arguments for a small standing army is not enough, even if one has living memories and inherited traditions as a guide. Throughout the early 20th century, as American political and sectional landscapes shifted, once-dominant ideas about the military and its relationship to American society constricted. What was once a dominant and cross-partisan perspective was polarized by the ideological reordering of the New Deal and the Second World War. The dissident camp was constrained further still as Northern Republicans converted in large numbers as a result of World War II, and a handful of stragglers saw the Korean War and the greater Cold War as a crisis that demanded the United States rethink its traditional reluctance to maintaining a large peacetime military.

In the decades since, what was once a norm became a memory and then became history.

Notes

1. Howard Buffett, "An Opportunity for the Republican Party," *New Individualist Review*, Summer 1962.

2. Charles H. Brand, "Volunteer System versus Conscription," extension of remarks, 65th Congress, 1st sess., Cong. Rec. 55 pt. 2, Appendix, 179 (1917).

3. Quoted in Michael Kazin, *War Against War: The American Fight for Peace, 1914–1918* (Simon & Schuster, 2017), p. 146.

4. Oswald Garrison Villard, "Preparedness Is Militarism," *New York Evening Post*, republished in *Annals of the American Academy of Political and Social Science* 66 (1916): 217–24.

5. For an argument that World War I created modern expectations of individual liberty, see Christopher Capozzola, *Uncle Sam Wants You: World War I and the Making of the Modern American Citizen* (Oxford University Press, 2008), pp. 156–57. For an authoritative account of the US government propaganda efforts via the Committee of Public Information, see John Maxwell Hamilton, *Manipulating the Masses: Woodrow Wilson and the Birth of American Propaganda* (Louisiana State University Press, 2020); Erika G. King, "Exposing the 'Age of Lies': The Propaganda Menace as Portrayed in American Magazines in the After-

math of World War I," *Journal of American Culture* 12, no. 1 (1989): 35–40; and Petra DeWitt, "'Clear and Present Danger': The Legacy of the 1917 Espionage Act in the United States," *Historical Reflections* 42, no. 2 (2016): 115–33. For domestic opposition to Woodrow Wilson's efforts to create a corporatized economy, see David M. Kennedy, *Over Here: The First World War and American Society* (Oxford University Press, 1982), chap. 1.

6. Oswald Garrison Villard, "The Newspaper and the Government," *Journalism Quarterly* 2 no. 3 (1925): 11–16.

7. Not to be confused with the libertarian magazine with the same title, *The Freeman*; quoted in King, "Exposing the 'Age of Lies,'" p. 37.

8. Quoted in King, "Exposing the 'Age of Lies,'" p. 38.

9. Theodore J. Zeman, "Military Interventions in the Coolidge Administration: Latin American and Asia," in *A Companion to Warren G. Harding, Calvin Coolidge, and Herbert Hoover*, ed. Katherine A. S. Sibley (John Wiley & Sons, Inc., 2014), pp. 273–274, 277; Anne L. Foster, *Projections of Power* (Duke University Press, 2010), pp. 20–21; and Charles A. Kupchan, *Isolationism: A History of America's Efforts to Shield Itself from the World* (Oxford University Press, 2020), pp. 260–61.

10. Justus D. Doenecke and John E. Wilz, *From Isolation to War: 1931–1941*, 3rd ed. (Harlan Davidson, 2003), p. 57. On the political influence of *Merchants of Death*, see Gerald Nye, "War Profits—The Profits of War and Preparedness," 74th Congress, 1st sess., Cong. Rec. 78, pt. 6, p. 6458. Gerald Nye, an erstwhile progressive supporter of American involvement in World War I, turned against the war and channeled his frustrations into a muckraking career as a local journalist. A war-induced agricultural bubble aided in his disillusionment and soured him on the idea of a federally managed economy. See Richard Aregood, Richard Shafer, and Eric Freedman, "American Isolationism and the Political Evolution of Journalist-Turned-US Senator Gerald Nye," *Journalism Practice* 9, no. 2 (2015).

11. Of those Southern Democrats who opposed American entry into the Great War, none served in Congress on the eve of the Second World War. Of those Democrats who opposed American entry into World War I, only South Carolina's former Rep. Frederick H. Dominick lived long enough to witness World War II. Forty-five Democrats who supported American entry into World War I served on the eve of American entry into World War II and were as a block supportive of FDR's preparedness efforts. For a look at President Woodrow Wilson's efforts to homogenize Southern politics and society, efforts that culminated in the South as a solid interventionist block on the eve of World War II, see Anthony Gaughan, "Woodrow Wilson and the Rise of Militant Interventionism in the South," *Journal of Southern History* 65, no. 4 (1999): 771–808.

12. See Ira Katznelson, *Fear Itself: The New Deal and the Origins of Our Time* (Liveright Publishing, 2013). Historian on noninterventionism Wayne S. Cole noted that the South was "strikingly resistant" to the activities of the America First Committee; see Wayne S. Cole, *America First: The Battle Against Intervention, 1940–1941* (Octagon Books, 1971), p. 31; Wayne S. Cole, *Charles A. Lindbergh and the Battle Against American Intervention in World War II* (Harcourt Brace Jovanovich, 1974), p. 11; and Wayne S. Cole, "America First and the South, 1940–1941," *Journal of Southern History* 22, no. 1 (1956): 36–47.

13. While the Democratic Party contained some prominent anti-war figures who voiced concerns about creating a large standing army and its effects on civil liberties, by 1941 that number was down to the single digits. Prominent Democratic anti-war voices Texas Rep. Murray Maverick and West Virginia Sen. Rush D. Holt were primaried. Both Maverick and Holt were ousted due to their respective positions on the New Deal, the former being primaried due to the influence of San Antonio's conservative political machine and the latter by the power of the United Mine Workers. On Maverick, see Stuart L. Weiss, "Maury Maverick and the Liberal Bloc," *Journal of American History* 57, no. 4 (1971): 880–95. On Holt, see William E. Coffey, "Isolationism and Pacifism: Senator Rush D. Holt and American Foreign Policy," *West Virginia History* 51 (1992): 1–14. Conversely, 20 Republicans who opposed American entry into World War I served into the waning days of American neutrality on the eve of World War II. Of those 20, only 4 showed signs of acquiescing to the demands of intervention and military preparedness, a remarkable element of ideological continuity that had no equal within the Democratic Party.

14. Robert A. Taft, "Is It Necessary to Draft Men?," 76th Congress, 3rd sess., Cong. Rec., vol. 86, pt. 10 5491.

15. Rose Wilder Lane, "We Who Have Sons," *Woman's Day*, December 1939, Rose Wilder Lane Papers, Box 44, Herbert Hoover Presidential Library and Museum, West Branch, Iowa.

16. Lane, "We Who Have Sons."

17. For an analysis of the 1942 midterms, see Thomas Fleming, *The New Dealers' War: FDR and the War Within World War II* (Basic Books, 2002), pp. 142–59; and Andrew E. Busch, *Horses in Midstream: U.S. Midterm Elections and Their Consequences* (University of Pittsburgh Press, 1999).

18. Howard Buffett to Herbert Hoover, January 20, 1936, in "Herbert Hoover's Fan from Omaha: Part I" by Thomas Schwartz, *Hoover Heads* (blog), archived January 2, 2024.

19. Howard Buffett, "Has 'Unconditional Surrender' Become Hitler's Most Deadly Weapon?" 79th Congress, 1st sess., Cong. Rec. 91, pt. 2, p. 2513.

20. Aaron L. Friedberg, *In the Shadow of the Garrison State: America's Anti-Statism and Its Cold War Grand Strategy* (Princeton University Press, 2000), pp. 80–86.

21. Michael J. Hogan, *A Cross of Iron: Harry S. Truman and the Origins of the National Security State* (Cambridge University Press, 1998), pp. 72–73.

22. Kupchan, *Isolationism*, p. 304.

23. Howard Buffett, "Washington Report," *Cook Chronicle*, May 14, 1948.

24. For an authoritative analysis of these noninterventionist holdouts and their opposition to the emerging Cold War state, see Justus D. Doenecke, *Not to the Swift: The Old Isolationists in the Cold War Era* (Associated University Presses, Inc., 1979); Hogan, *A Cross of Iron*; and Friedberg, *In the Shadow of the Garrison State*.

25. See Joyce Mao, *Asia First: China and the Making of the Modern Conservative Movement* (University of Chicago Press, 2015). Mao argues that crises in China and Korea, as well as long-standing American interests in the Pacific, were central to the transformation of conservative foreign policy perspectives.

26. For information on the conversion of Arthur Vandenberg and his role as a Republican shepherd of the early national security state, see Doenecke, *Not to the Swift*, p. 10; Colin Dueck, *Hard Line: The Republican Party and U.S. Foreign Policy Since World War II* (Princeton University Press, 2010), p. 73; Ronald Radosh, *Prophets on the Right: Profiles of Conservative Critics of American Globalism* (Simon & Schuster, 1975), p. 154; and David Pietrusza, *1948: Harry Truman's Improbable Victory and the Year That Transformed America* (Union Square Press, 2011), pp. 88–89.

27. National Security Act of 1947, Pub. L. No. 80-235, 61 Stat. 496.

28. Chiperfield also evolved on foreign policy as he was one of seven Republicans who opposed the Greece-Turkey aid bill but came to support the Mutual Security Act, legislation that globalized the logic of the Cold War. According to political science data from Keith T. Poole and Howard Rosenthal, the seven Republicans who had converted by the Korean War averaged a combined ideological score of −0.303, considerably more liberal than the Republican Party average in the 81st Congress, or those who maintain their opposition on foreign aid. Drawn from original research of the NOMINATE dataset, Jeffrey B. Lewis, Keith Poole, Howard Rosenthal, Adam Boche, Aaron Rudkin, and Luke Sonnet, data from VoteView, Congressional Roll-Call Votes Database, 2025. See Brandan P. Buck, "Partisans of the Old Republic: Right-Wing Opposition to U.S. Foreign Policy" (PhD diss., George Mason University, 2024), p. 128–29. ProQuest, Order No. 31336256).

29. Rep. Robert Chiperfield (R-IL), U.S. Congress, House, Committee, *Draft Legislation to Amend Further the Mutual Security Act of 1954, As Amended, and for Other Purposes*, 86th Cong., 1st sess., 1959, p. 966.

30. Murray N. Rothbard, edited by Thomas E. Woods, Jr., *The Betrayal of the American Right* (Ludwig von Mises Institute, 2007), p. 93

31. Howard Buffett, "The Evil Men in the Kremlin Must Be Chortling as Militarism Runs Wild in America," 82nd Congress, 2nd sess., Cong. Rec. 98, pt. 1 A734.

32. Howard Buffett, "Washington Report," *Alexandria Argus*, February 21, 1952.

33. The former president turned conservative fixer, Herbert Hoover, captured this mood when he advised "arming to the teeth" coupled with a "policy of watchful waiting," as he had on the eve of World War II. Herbert Hoover to Felix Morley, December 18, 1952; Herbert Hoover, Folder, Box 1, Felix Morley Papers, Herbert Hoover Presidential Library, West Branch, Iowa. Robert A. Taft also advocated for a hemispheric defense policy in his campaign tract, *A Foreign Policy for Americans* (Doubleday & Company, 1951), pp. 74–75. While such approaches were not alien to conservative or noninterventionist politics—and were derived from a pre–World War II conception of "Fortress America" at the center of a Western Hemisphere bounded by the Monroe Doctrine—they weakened the larger coalition opposing the maximalist aims of the emerging Cold War consensus.

34. Hogan, *A Cross of Iron*, pp. 265, 319. See also Friedberg, *In the Shadow of the Garrison State*, pp. 130–32. Fifty-six Republican representatives and senators had careers that spanned the period from America's entry into World War II to the start of the Eisenhower administration. Even prominent noninterventionist House Republicans, such as Noah Mason (R-IL), Usher Burdick (R-ND), and

Clare Hoffman (R-MI), who had displayed a dogged opposition to military preparedness on the eve of World War II, acquiesced to the demands of the New Look. By the 84th Congress, the second that served alongside the Eisenhower administration and the first with a full suite of defense legislation, not a single Republican voted in opposition to said legislation more than 50 percent of the time. In the 84th Congress, total Republican opposition to defense legislation averaged 37 percent, only marginally higher than the Democrats, at 29 percent.

35. H. R. Gross to Howard Buffett, March 26, 1963, Buffett, Howard Folder, H. R. Gross Papers, Herbert Hoover Presidential Library, West Branch, Iowa.

36. Howard Buffett to H. R. Gross, March 1, 1963, Howard Folder, H. R. Gross Papers, Herbert Hoover Presidential Library, West Branch, Iowa.

37. Howard Buffett to H. R. Gross, March 13, 1963, Howard Folder, H. R. Gross Papers, Herbert Hoover Presidential Library, West Branch, Iowa. Buffett referred to rollcall vote six, on H.R. 2438, March 11, 1963.

38. H. R. Gross to Howard Buffett, March 26, 1963.

39. For more on Flexible Response and the realignment of defense policy under Kennedy, see Campbell Craig and Fredrik Logevall, *America's Cold War: The Politics of Insecurity* (Belknap Press of Harvard University Press, 2009); David Halberstam, *The Best and the Brightest* (Ballantine Books, 1969); and Arne Odd Westad, *The Global Cold War* (Cambridge University Press, 2007). A handful of congressional conservatives opposed JFK's efforts to expand defense spending and capacities beyond nuclear deterrence on fiscal and strategic grounds, but they were too few to stop those policies. See "Congress Cuts Defense Funds $1.8 Billion," in *CQ Almanac* (1963), 19th ed. (Congressional Quarterly, 1964), pp. 141–46.

40. *New Individualist Review*, while under the editorship of Milton Friedman, published a special all-conscription edition in the spring of 1967 that included essays from rising libertarian stars like Jim Powell and Joe Michael Cobb as well as older materials from Old Right figures such as Robert A. Taft. For more on Friedman's role in ending the draft, see Beth Bailey, "The Army in the Marketplace: Recruiting an All-Volunteer Force," *Journal of American History* 94, no. 1 (2007): 47–74; Brian Doherty, *Radicals for Capitalism: A Freewheeling History of the Modern American Libertarian Movement* (PublicAffairs, 2007), p. 372; and John D. Singleton, "Slaves or Mercenaries? Milton Friedman and the Institution of the All-Volunteer Military," in *Milton Friedman: Contributions to Economics and Public Policy*, ed. Robert A. Cord and J. Daniel Hammond (Oxford University Press, 2016).

7

THE FOUNDERS' TRADE GRIEVANCES—AND TODAY'S

DOUGLAS A. IRWIN

For cutting off our Trade with all Parts of the World:

"No taxation without representation!" was one of the rallying cries of the American independence movement in the 1770s. The taxation in question was partly that on foreign trade. Among the many grievances cited in the Declaration of Independence was the complaint about Britain "cutting off our Trade with all Parts of the World" and "imposing taxes on us without our consent."

While the conflict between Britain and the 13 North American colonies was ultimately about political power and sovereignty, many specific disputes concerned the restrictions and taxes that Britain imposed on colonial commerce. This chapter briefly reviews those complaints and the role they played in driving the colonial demands for independence. Once the United States achieved independence, however, the country had to grapple with how to structure its own trade policies based on domestic considerations. That led to new grievances that had to be mediated in Washington rather than London.

Trade Regulation and the Navigation Acts

For more than a century after the first permanent English settlement in North America was established at Jamestown in 1607, the New World settlers were heavily dependent on foreign trade. Trade was essential to the well-being of the colonists, furnishing them with clothing and blankets, nails and firearms, cooking implements and metal goods, and other tools and materials that could not be produced locally. Without these imports, the colonists' standard of living might have suffered so much that they would not have stayed. As historians John J. McCusker and Russell R. Menard put it, "Overseas commerce did not merely make colonial life comfortable, it made it possible."[1]

Although the share and variety of goods in America's foreign trade was largely determined by regional resource endowments and driven by market forces, the geographic pattern of trade was not. The British Parliament enacted the Navigation Acts, which artificially channeled colonial trade through Britain and its territories in the West Indies.

The purpose of the Navigation Acts was to promote Britain's maritime power and ensure that trade within the empire served its commercial interests. First applied to the American colonies in 1651, the Navigation Acts involved a complex web of government policies. These mercantilist policies—designed to promote British commercial interests by promoting exports and restricting imports—regulated the nationality of the ships and crews employed in British and colonial commerce (akin to the Jones Act today); restricted the destinations to which colonial goods could be shipped and the sources of colonial imports; favored certain British industries with subsidies, preferential tariffs, charter monopolies, and other encouragements; and prohibited the development of certain industries in the colonies that might harm producers in Britain.

From America's standpoint, the most important regulation was the requirement that almost all its exports and imports be shipped via Britain. In terms of exports, all "enumerated" goods had to pass through a British port before reaching their final destination.

About three-quarters of American exports were enumerated, the most important of which was tobacco. Most tobacco exports were not destined for Britain but reexported to Europe. The indirect routing through Britain imposed extra costs on American exporters and reduced the prices received by tobacco planters. If tobacco had not been enumerated and could have been sold directly to European customers, the income of tobacco planters would have been anywhere from 15 to 35 percent higher, estimates historian Larry Sawers.[2] Thus, the Navigation laws imposed a significant burden on a politically influential, trade-dependent group, the Chesapeake tobacco farmers of Maryland and Virginia.

The Navigation Acts did not significantly distort colonial imports. Most of America's imports from Britain were made in Britain, the world's leading producer of manufactured goods. For some of these goods, such as gunpowder, linen, sailcloth, silk, and refined sugar, the colonies benefited from British export subsidies that lowered their price to American consumers. However, most non-British imports, whether from Europe or Asia, first had to be shipped through Britain.

This artificial routing through Britain involved extra fees, commissions, warehouse rents, and transportation costs and is estimated to have raised the costs of imports of European and Asian goods by about 20 percent. In a pioneering calculation, Lawrence Harper in 1939 tallied the costs and benefits to the colonies from these trade restrictions for the year 1773. He estimated the total cost to be $3.3 million, only about 2 percent of colonial income. The enumeration of tobacco was by far the largest component, accounting for three-quarters of the total cost.[3] Robert Paul Thomas in 1965 revised Harper's calculation down to $2.7 million but also took account of the colonial benefits of being part of the British Empire.[4] These benefits were estimated to be $1.8 million and arose in part due to the lower insurance rates on shipping because of the protection provided by the Royal Navy. In this broader calculation, the net cost to the colonies came to just $0.9 million, a slight 0.6 percent of colonial income. As McCusker and Menard conclude, "Whatever the costs of membership in the British Empire, they were largely offset by the benefits: naval protection; access to a large free-trading area; easy credit and cheap manufactures; and restricted foreign competition."[5]

The fact that the aggregate burden of Britain's commercial policies on the colonies was small, however, does not mean that these restrictions were unimportant in spurring demands for independence. Only a minority of the colonial population is believed to have actively supported independence in 1776, and this vocal and politically powerful minority may have been precisely those most affected by Britain's trade policies. In fact, about 90 percent of the economic burden of the Navigation laws is believed to have fallen upon the Southern colonies, particularly tobacco planters in Maryland and Virginia, and might have reduced the region's income by as much as 2.5 percent in 1770.[6]

It was not a coincidence that these planters strongly supported independence. Virginians believed that freeing the tobacco trade from Britain's commercial regulations would make the crop much more profitable. Indeed, in the 1640s, Virginia's House of Burgesses petitioned for a "free export of their Tobacco to foreign Markets directly," although their request was rejected by the British Privy Council. In 1774, in a draft of instructions to its delegates to the Continental Congress, the Virginia legislature declared that "the exercise of a free trade with all parts of the world, possessed by the American colonists as of natural right, and which no law of their own had taken away or abridged" was a subject of "unjust incroachment" by the British authorities.[7]

Another group that held grievances against British policy consisted of urban merchants in Boston, New York, and Philadelphia. These merchants were also dismayed by British commercial regulations that restricted their freedom to trade with other regions of the world. "The merchants of revolutionary America made up but a very small part of the population, but they wielded economic and political power within most of the Colonies far out of proportion to their numbers," Merrill Jensen notes. By contrast, farmers who made up the bulk of the population "did not share the economic grievances of either merchants and tradesmen of the coastal cities or of the tobacco growing planters of Virginia and Maryland" and only later supported the movement toward independence.[8]

In sum, the colonies were not impoverished and exploited victims of British rule. The cost of British mercantilist trade regulations was roughly offset by the benefits of protection within the British Empire. In fact, the colonies had conducted their business under the Navigation Acts without complaint for more than a century and had flourished as a result. In his 1951 review of contemporary writings, the historian Oliver M. Dickerson could not find any evidence that the

Navigation Acts or Britain's commercial policies were a major source of complaint in the colonial assemblies.[9] At the same time, such trade regulations did adversely affect certain groups, particularly tobacco farmers. They and others were to become among the most vocal proponents of independence and to play a catalytic role in the drive for national sovereignty.

Taxes, Taxes, Taxes

With the colonies generally prospering under British rule, something must have changed to bring about the resistance that ultimately led to revolution. That change began after the end of the Seven Years' War in 1763, when Britain attempted to institute new policies that the colonists believed would threaten their comfortable state.

The Seven Years War, known as the French and Indian War in North America, was undertaken in large part to protect the colonies from neighboring threats. The war proved to be very expensive, increasing the British government's debt from less than £80 million in 1757 to £134 million in 1764. The annual interest on this debt amounted to nearly £5 million at a time when the government's annual revenue was only about £9 million.[10]

The British government also had to pay the considerable ongoing cost of protecting the newly enlarged North American territories. As a result of its victory, Britain acquired a huge amount of land—not just most of North America east of the Mississippi River, but Canada and parts of the West Indies as well—and it all needed to be defended. The cost of maintaining a standing army of 10,000 soldiers in North America amounted to nearly 4 percent of the British government's budget.[11] With the external threat of the French and Indians having been removed, Americans failed to appreciate the substantial costs that Britain incurred in defending the colonies.

After 1763, British policy aimed to extract revenue from the colonies to pay for these costs. This policy shift implied a major increase in the tax burden on the colonies. Given the colonies' economic size and geographic location, as well as the fact that expenses had been and were being incurred on their behalf, British officials naturally thought that the colonists should contribute more to the costs of defense and the servicing of debts. Therefore, successive British administrations sought to raise additional revenues from what they viewed as the wealthy and undertaxed American colonies.

To the dismay of the British authorities, most of the measures they enacted were met with stiff resistance. While most colonists accepted Britain's longstanding regulation of America's trade, they resisted British attempts to put more of the financial burden of supporting the colonies on the colonists themselves. By discounting the benefits of protection within the British Empire, the colonists saw the new taxes and regulations as a threat to their prosperity and future well-being.

The Sugar Act of 1764 required that the colonies pay a three-shilling duty on sugar and molasses imported from places other than the British West Indies. This was half of the official duty that dated back to 1733, but that tax had been routinely ignored by American merchants and British customs officials. The customs service was also reinvigorated to better enforce existing laws to reduce smuggling and increase revenue. These measures generated grumbles in the colonies, but no outright opposition.

The Stamp Act of 1765 levied duties on public documents and printed materials, such as legal documents, newspapers, property deeds, and playing cards. Although such taxes were common in Britain, these new internal taxes provoked sharp protests in the colonies. Residents of the commercial colonies, principally Massachusetts and New York, argued that they had not been properly represented in Parliament, and therefore they could not accept such internal taxation. They acknowledged that Britain had the authority to regulate the empire's foreign trade but rejected the attempt to impose internal taxes without the colonies' consent. Parliament rejected the distinction between external and internal taxes and asserted that it had the power to impose any taxes it chose.

The Stamp Act Congress, the first joint meeting of representatives of all the colonies initiated on their own, sought to formulate a unified response to the British action. In October 1765, colonial delegates adopted a Declaration of Rights, which stated that taxes should not be imposed without their consent and noted that "the restrictions imposed . . . on the trade of these colonies will render them unable to purchase the manufactures of Great Britain."[12]

The colonies also agreed to try to force Britain to repeal the Stamp Act through commercial pressure in the form of nonimportation agreements among colonial merchants. The leaders of the boycott thought that the lost sales would force British exporters to lobby on their behalf in London. The impact of the colonial boycott of British goods is uncertain because nonimportation lasted just a few months and coincided with a general economic slowdown. The volume of America's imports from Britain fell by seven percent in 1766, after having fallen by 14 percent in 1765, making it hard to disentangle the impact of nonimportation from the recession in reducing trade.[13] The falloff in North American orders was keenly felt in Britain, which was also experiencing an economic downturn, and British merchants flooded Parliament with petitions describing the hardship and loss of employment arising from cancellations of American orders for their goods.

Even if the economic impact of nonimportation was modest compared with the recession, the political impact was large enough that the protesters achieved their objective: Pressure from British manufacturers was an important factor in Parliament's decision to repeal the Stamp Act in early 1766. Recognizing that the Stamp Act and sugar duties were generating little revenue and much ill will, Parliament repealed both measures in March 1766. The nonimportation movement quickly collapsed once word of the repeal arrived in the colonies.

However, along with the repeal, Parliament also passed the Declaratory Act, which asserted Parliament's full power and authority to make laws and govern the colonies and reiterated its legal right to tax both external and internal commerce. With Britain still desperate to tap into the colonial economy as a source of revenue, the new chancellor of the exchequer, Charles Townshend, proposed establishing customs commissioners in the major colonial port cities to strengthen the enforcement of the customs laws and ensure the collection of import duties. Townshend also proposed a new set of low duties on many different commodities to discourage smuggling and the evasion of duties. Townshend was careful to ensure that these duties were imposed on external trade and did not include the objectionable internal taxes.

Yet the Townshend measures, which included the controversial policy of quartering soldiers in private homes, provoked even greater colonial resistance than the Sugar Act had. Once again, British policy triggered a trade boycott. This time, as opposition to Townshend's policies brewed, civic leaders, rather than city merchants, orchestrated the movement for the nonimportation or nonconsumption of British goods. This second nonimportation movement only emerged gradually and unequally across the colonies. Still, the overall volume of imports from Britain dropped 38 percent in 1769.[14]

By this time, yet another British ministry—noting that the duties were again failing to raise much revenue but had stoked popular resentment—backed off. In April 1770, Parliament repealed the Townshend duties, except for the one on tea, which had raised three-quarters of the revenue. The leaders of the American nonimportation movement strenuously argued that the boycott should continue until the duty on tea was abolished as well. But merchants could not resist taking advantage of the British repeal as an excuse to resume trade and, like its predecessor, the second nonimportation movement quickly collapsed.

A pattern had been established: New British taxes were imposed, sparking a nonimportation movement in America, leading to a British retreat. The colonists drew the conclusion—correctly in the case of the Stamp Act but incorrectly in the case of the Townshend duties—that British policy could be manipulated with American trade embargoes. The colonists took from this experience an exaggerated impression of their ability to coerce British policy through economic means. In fact, nonimportation only had a significant impact when it coincided with an economic downturn in Britain; the colonies could have only a modest influence on the country because just 15 percent of British exports were destined for America in 1765.[15]

New Conflict

From 1770 until early 1773, trans-Atlantic relations were eerily calm. During this period, the colonial grievances festered, but the British government did not undertake any new actions that might become a rallying cry for protest. Then an economic crisis hit Virginia while a new Tea Act inflamed Massachusetts.

In the South, Virginia planters, already weighed down by heavy debts and resentful of the control of their trade by Scottish agents, faced a devastating collapse in tobacco prices in 1772 and 1773. The trigger was a financial crisis in Britain that quickly made its way to the colonies. Tobacco prices dropped by half, and credit to Virginia and Maryland planters was tightened. The debt burden of tidewater planters soared, leading to a wave of foreclosures and imprisonment. The catastrophe intensified anti-British sentiment, and Chesapeake planters imagined that their financial prospects would be brighter if only they were free to sell their produce to the world market directly, instead of through Britain as the Navigation laws required.

The Tea Act, passed by Parliament in early 1773, also put the colonies back in confrontation with Britain. This legislation aimed to help bail out the financially troubled East India Company by giving it a monopoly on tea sales in the colonies. The British government also sought to undercut smugglers—two-thirds of the tea consumed in America was believed to have been smuggled to avoid paying any duty—by slashing the import duty on tea and allowing the company to transport cargo directly to North America without stopping in Britain. The revenue implications of bringing the smuggled tea into legal channels of trade and taxing it were enormous.

Even though Britain was actually reducing the price of legal tea imports, colonial merchants—many of whom were probably complicit in the illegal smuggling—protested the granting of a monopoly privilege to the East India Company and the payment of duty. They succeeded in riling up other colonists against the British action, and, in the fall of 1773, American ports began turning away East India ships loaded with tea. In Boston, several ships landed but were not permitted to unload. At the instigation of local merchants who profited from smuggled tea, crowds gathered near the docks on December 16, 1773. About 150 people stormed an East India Company ship and dumped 342 chests of tea (about 90,000 pounds) into the harbor. Thus, the famous Boston Tea Party was not a protest about an unfair tax increase, since the duty was actually being reduced, but about a British attempt to make the smuggling of tea unprofitable so that the East India Company could gain control of the trade.[16]

Collision Course for War

Outraged by these events, British officials passed the Coercive Acts (known as the Intolerable Acts in America) in the spring of 1774. These measures closed the port of Boston until the destroyed tea had been paid for, gave the royal governor direct authority over the local government, and required the colonies to provide housing and provisions for British soldiers. Britain and the 13 North America colonies were now on a collision course.

The colonies banded together in the First Continental Congress, which convened during September and October of 1774. The Congress denied Parliament's jurisdiction over the domestic affairs of the colonies, except as it pertained to the regulation of foreign trade, and pointedly rejected internal taxation without representation. The Congress issued the Declaration of Rights and Grievances, which explained that the colonists "cheerfully consent to the operation of such acts of the British parliament, as are bona fide restrained to the regulation of our external commerce, for the purpose of securing the commercial advantages of the whole empire to the mother country," but excluded "every idea of taxation, internal or external, for raising a revenue on the subjects in America without their consent." But, the declaration continued, the colonists were "entitled to life, liberty, & property, and they have never ceded to any sovereign power whatever, a right to dispose of either without their consent."[17]

The colonies essentially wanted a return to Britain's pre-1763 benign neglect with regard to their internal affairs. They also requested the repeal of many laws enacted after 1763, but not the Tea Act, which it accepted as part of the Navigation Acts. The Congress called for the nonimportation of all goods from Britain, Ireland, and the British West Indies starting in December 1774 until the Coercive Acts had been repealed. After issuing these demands, the representatives adjourned until May 1775 and awaited the British response.

Britain opted for a military solution. In early 1775, the government declared Massachusetts to be in a state of rebellion and sent its armed forces to occupy Boston, leading to the clashes at Lexington and Concord. In May, Congress decided to augment nonimportation with nonexportation: A ban on all exports to Britain and the West Indies started a year later.

The national embargo on trade with Britain had a much more pronounced effect on trade than had the previous nonimportation movement. Imports from Britain essentially evaporated in 1775. Exports rose in 1775 as American farmers and planters strained to make as many last shipments to Britain as possible but then disappeared the following year. By this time, fighting had broken out between British and colonial forces in Massachusetts, and the colonies began to move toward independence in the spring of 1776.

Independence to Today

The Revolutionary War was concluded, and the United States won its independence, with the Treaty of Paris in September 1783. But the 1780s were a difficult time for the new nation. The United States lost its preferential trading status within the British Empire, meaning that trade volumes were lower than before the war. For an economy that still depended on foreign trade, this was an economic blow. In addition, America's governing document, the Articles of Confederation, did not allow the national government to regulate trade or impose taxes on trade. Consequently, the government was broke: It could not raise revenue and fund the debt, provide for the national defense, or fund its current operations. (Voluntary contributions from the states had fallen to a trickle by the end of the decade.)

The nation's precarious fiscal future provided the impetus for a new constitution in 1789 that gave Congress the power to regulate and tax foreign trade (Article I, Section 8). In a nod to Southern plantation owners, who wanted their tobacco and cotton to be sold unimpeded to foreign markets, export taxes were expressly prohibited. The second act passed by the new government under President George Washington was a tariff act that levied duties on imports to generate revenue and fund government expenses.

In subsequent decades, deciding on the level of import tariffs was for Washington, not London, to do. Finding a domestic consensus on tariffs was never easy. In *Federalist* no. 10, James Madison anticipated that tariffs would become a major political issue for Congress. Setting tariffs was an inherently political exercise in which many domestic interests were in play. "A landed interest, a manufacturing interest, a mercantile interest, a moneyed interest, with many lesser interests, grow up of necessity in civilized nations, and divide them into different classes, actuated by different sentiments and views," Madison wrote. "The regulation of these various and interfering interests forms the principal task of modern legislation and involves the spirit of party and faction in the necessary and ordinary operations of the government."[18]

Tariffs were initially imposed to raise revenue. Prior to the Civil War, tariffs raised about 90 percent of federal government revenue. But tariffs also pitted domestic manufacturers who were competing against foreign producers (and hence wanted high import tariffs) against domestic farmers who were seeking to export their products to foreign markets (and hence wanted low import tariffs).

This led to a sharp geographic split concerning trade. In Congress, representatives from Northern states, which were the home of nascent manufacturing industries such as textiles and steel, voted for high tariffs to keep out imports. Representatives from Southern states, whose economies relied on exported crops such as tobacco and cotton, voted for lower tariffs to expand trade. This voting pattern was evident as early as the 1790s and continued through the middle of the 20th century.[19] In the 1820s, South Carolina sought to nullify the high tariffs of that period and even threatened to secede from the Union, raising a trade policy dispute into a constitutional crisis.

The Civil War brought the Republican Party, whose political support came from the North, into political power for many decades. As a result, average tariffs on dutiable imports were set at about 30–40 percent over the objections of Democrats from the South. Tariffs were not used for revenue, particularly after the introduction of the income tax in 1913, as much as to restrict imports to help domestic producers compete against foreign goods.[20]

The Great Depression of the 1930s brought a political realignment in favor of the Democrats. They exacted the Reciprocal Trade Agreements Act of 1934, in which Congress delegated to the president the power to negotiate agreements with other countries to reduce tariffs. This approach was energized after World War II, when the United

States led the world into such agreements as the General Agreement on Tariffs and Trade, which began to reduce tariffs among participating countries (and in 1995 was replaced by the World Trade Organization). By the end of the 20th century, the average tariff on dutiable imports was less than 5 percent and the United States had many free trade agreements with countries around the world, including Canada and Mexico. The creation of the World Trade Organization in 1995 seemed to solidify this move.

Yet US trade policy moved in another direction with the election of Donald Trump as president in 2016. Believing that other countries had been taking advantage of the open US market, President Trump sought to increase tariffs on imports from all countries, particularly in his second term in office. This controversial action simply showed that the trade debate in the United States, which goes back to the colonial period, has never really ended.

Conclusion

Controversy about authority over trade policy was bound up with the demands for political independence at the very start of the country. "The dispute between Britain and the colonies was not over Parliament's right to regulate this or that trade, to tax a particular activity, or to pursue a specific policy," McCusker and Menard conclude. "The conflict centered on the issue of power over the long haul, on the shape of things to come, on who would determine the future of the British Empire in the Americas."[21]

When the United States gained independence from Britain in 1783, it gained the power to set its own tariff. The subsequent 250 years, however, have shown that determining trade policy involves sharp domestic divisions and trade-offs that are constantly being reassessed.

Notes

1. John J. McCusker and Russell R. Menard, *The Economy of British America, 1607–1789* (University of North Carolina Press, 1985), p. 71.
2. Larry Sawers, "The Navigation Acts Revisited," *Economic History Review* 45, no. 2 (May 1992): 281–82.
3. Lawrence A. Harper, *The English Navigation Laws: A Seventeenth-Century Experiment in Social Engineering* (Columbia University Press, 1939).

4. Robert Paul Thomas, "A Quantitative Approach to the Study of the Effects of British Imperial Policy upon Colonial Welfare: Some Preliminary Findings," *Journal of Economic History* 25, no. 4 (1965): 615–38.

5. McCusker and Menard, *The Economy of British America*, p. 354.

6. Roger L. Ransom, "British Policy and Colonial Growth: Some Implications of the Burden from the Navigation Acts," *Journal of Economic History* 28, no. 3 (1968): 427–35.

7. Julian Boyd, ed. *The Papers of Thomas Jefferson* Vol. 1, *January 1760 to December 1776* (Princeton University Press, 1950), p. 123.

8. Merrill Jensen, "The American Revolution and American Agriculture," *Agricultural History* 43, no. 1 (1969): 109.

9. Oliver M. Dickerson, *The Navigation Acts and the American Revolution* (University of Pennsylvania Press, 1951).

10. B. R. Mitchell, *British Historical Statistics* (Cambridge University Press, 1988), p. 579.

11. P. D. G. Thomas, *The Townshend Duties Crisis: The Second Phase of the American Revolution, 1767–1773* (Oxford University Press, 1987).

12. Resolutions of the Continental Congress, October 19, 1765, The Avalon Project: Documents in Law, History, and Diplomacy.

13. US Bureau of the Census, *Historical Statistics of the United States: Bicentennial Edition*, chap. Z (Government Printing Office, 1975), pp. 127–28.

14. Douglas A. Irwin, *Clashing over Commerce: A History of US Trade Policy* (University of Chicago Press, 2017), p. 42.

15. Irwin, *Clashing over Commerce*, p. 42.

16. Benjamin W. Labree, *The Boston Tea Party* (Oxford University Press, 1964).

17. Declaration and Resolves of the First Continental Congress, October 14, 1774, The Avalon Project: Documents in Law, History, and Diplomacy.

18. James Madison, "The Same Subject Continued: The Union as a Safeguard Against Domestic Faction and Insurrection," *Federalist* no. 10, *New York Packet*, November 23, 1787.

19. Irwin, *Clashing over Commerce.*

20. Madison, *Federalist* no. 10.

21. McCusker and Menard, *The Economy of British America*, p. 357.

8

A HISTORY OF GOVERNMENT BY EXECUTIVE ORDER

BRENT SKORUP

He has dissolved Representative Houses repeatedly, for opposing with manly Firmness his Invasions on the Rights of the People.

Executive orders issued by the president often affect the rights and liberty of millions of people. In recent years, such orders have set—and frequently reversed—federal policy and priorities on politically salient topics, including immigration, COVID-19 vaccines, "racial equity," and women's sports. Throughout American history, executive orders have initiated significant programs and legal precedents. Presidents have used them to suspend habeas corpus nationwide,[1] desegregate the military,[2] create a system of concentration camps for citizens during World War II,[3] and authorize warrantless collection of millions of Americans' digital communications.[4]

For all their significance, executive orders have an ambiguous constitutional status. The Constitution vests all legislative power in Congress.[5] It also charges the president with the duty to "take care that the laws be faithfully executed."[6] In theory, then, the president has no power to make law, only the power to sign and enforce laws passed by Congress and, when necessary, to administer them. Many laws require an administrator to make judgments about the application of the laws, and since the nation's founding, every president has issued executive orders and statements to guide the actions of his subordinates in the executive branch.[7]

However, modern presidents have exercised immense discretion that often functions identically to—and even displaces—lawmaking by Congress. There was a distinct increase in the exercise of executive power and the use of executive orders in 1933 when President Franklin Delano Roosevelt took office. Today, most "functional lawmaking" by the president—and his executive branch subordinates—takes the form of regulations issued by executive branch agencies, like the Departments of Commerce, the Treasury, and Energy. But the use of executive orders, along with related instruments like proclamations, memoranda, "notices," and "directives" (collectively, "executive orders"), has grown noticeably in the past 20 years. Executive orders are powerful, and they appeal to presidents largely because their issuance is not constrained by bicameralism, presentment, and constraints on administrative agencies like the Administrative Procedure Act.[8]

Some businesses, organizations, and individuals have fought back against broad assertions of executive power. When President Harry Truman attempted to seize steel plants during wartime in 1952, the mill owners challenged the takeover and the Supreme Court rejected the attempted seizures.[9] The Supreme Court held in *Youngstown Sheet & Tube Co. v. Sawyer*: "The President's power, if any, to issue [an] order must stem either from an act of Congress or from the Constitution itself."[10] While that appears to be a severe constraint, the following examples starkly illustrate those constraints' ephemerality.[11] Time and again, vague statutory references and unspecified constitutional powers cited in executive orders have been used to justify sweeping assertions of government power into Americans' lives, livelihoods, and property.

Executive Orders Before 1933

It is difficult to make generalizations about the thousands (estimates vary) of executive orders, given their varied purposes.[12] The most notable use of executive orders in the 19th century came from President Abraham Lincoln during the Civil War. In April 1861, a few weeks after Confederate forces fired upon Fort Sumter in South Carolina, Lincoln feared the Maryland legislature might arm its people against the United States. In anticipation, Lincoln instructed a military official in Maryland to "bombard[] . . . their cities and, in the extremist necessity," suspend the writ of habeas corpus.[13] Two days later he authorized his top general to suspend habeas corpus in Philadelphia and Washington,[14] then expanded that instruction twice more to cover most Northern cities.[15] Notably, he did not cite constitutional or statutory authorizations for the executive orders.

However, President Lincoln's use of executive orders and contested assertions of presidential power were an anomaly in the 19th century. At the time, executive orders were rare and most were limited to administrative functions—such as notifying employees of a prominent politician's death or directing government officials to carry out laws passed by Congress.[16] They ranged from planning public grounds in the District of Columbia to leasing public lands to industry to endorsing the reinstatement of certain people to employment in the federal government.[17]

Still, after the Civil War the use of executive orders increased somewhat, and some trends are evident. From 1870 to 1885, and again during President William Howard Taft's administration from 1909 to 1913, most executive orders concerned the demarcation of lands for Indian tribes. From 1885 to 1897, after the passage of the Pendleton Act of 1883 and its reform of the "spoils" system, Presidents Grover Cleveland and Benjamin Harrison issued dozens of rules for civil service employment and practices.[18]

However, President Theodore Roosevelt initiated an increase in the use of executive orders, prompting the State Department in 1907 to assign each order a number.[19] President Woodrow Wilson continued this trend, creating entire agencies by executive order, including the War Trade Board, the Grain Corporation, and the Food Administration.[20] Presidents have used executive orders liberally in times of real and perceived national emergencies ever since.

The 1930s: Emergency and a New Era of Executive Power

The growing power of the president in recent decades is closely tied to emergencies—real, perceived, and invented. During the Great Depression, the Supreme Court said in *Home Building & Loan Ass'n v. Blaisdell* that emergencies "furnish the occasion for the exercise" of novel and never-before-used government powers.[21] Unsurprisingly, perhaps, America has been under president-declared states of emergency nearly continuously since the *Blaisdell* decision and, presently, there are dozens of national emergencies in effect.[22]

President Franklin Roosevelt inaugurated a new era in using executive orders, including nearly 1,500 in his first term. One of his first was to answer an emergency—the weakness and failure of many US banks in the winter of 1932 and 1933. Two days after taking office, on March 6, 1933, Roosevelt relied on an interpretation of a wartime law, the Trading with the Enemy Act, to proclaim a bank holiday—a purported peacetime emergency.[23] The president's interpretation was dubious—the 1917 law only granted emergency powers to the president "compatible with . . . the successful prosecution of the war."[24]

Nevertheless, rather than reassert its authority to write laws in the face of Roosevelt's effective rewriting of statutes, Congress responded within days to ratify the president's new power with the Emergency Banking Act.[25] The House passed the bill after only 38 minutes of debate, and members had no printed copies of the bill available for study and debate.[26] The Senate approved the legislation later that evening. The law expanded presidential authority immensely "to provide relief in the existing national emergency in banking, and for other purposes."[27] It also removed a 1917 restriction that limited the president's financial regulatory power over transactions involving foreign parties. As one economic historian noted, "Absolute control of money dealings, foreign and domestic, thereafter required not an act of Congress but only a national emergency as a president saw fit to declare."[28]

Broad claims of executive power can have a cascading effect, creating more emergencies that justify the use of executive power.[29] For instance, after the president used these new powers to place banks under federal supervision and to largely prohibit them from paying out gold to bank customers, another emergency quickly followed.[30]

Weeks later, after Americans—predictably—tried to withdraw their gold from their banks, the president cited his emergency powers again to prohibit gold "hoarding" and ordered Americans to surrender all of their gold and gold certificates to their nearest bank.[31] The order provided that Americans who refused to forfeit their gold in these compelled transactions faced $10,000 penalties—exceeding $250,000 in 2025 dollars—and up to 10 years in prison.[32]

Congress acquiesced to—and even encouraged—FDR's expansion of executive power. In the months and years that followed, Congress proceeded to give the president and his delegates immense authority, including to reduce agricultural production,[33] reorganize the executive branch,[34] and cartelize nearly every industry in the United States.[35] Then to prepare the nation for entry into World War II, the president used these powers and executive orders to seize an aviation plant,[36] assign public land for aerial bombing training,[37] and (during the joint German-Soviet invasions of their neighbors) seize the assets of German and Soviet officials and their affiliates in occupied countries.[38]

Legal Dark Matter

Much like dark matter in physics—unseen but massively influential—emergency executive powers lie dormant until activated, often with sweeping consequences. These powers spring forth only upon their exercise but often persist because they have tremendous inertia. For instance, presidents today still cite, as President Franklin Roosevelt did, the Trading with the Enemy Act—a World War I relic designed to freeze the assets of Germany and Austria-Hungary—to seize foreigners' assets and sanction entire nations. Another alarming aspect of this legal dark matter is that the combination of latent emergency powers and excessive congressional delegation to the executive branch via broad and vague legislation means that it is often impossible for a normal person or legislator to know how an executive order—or codified law—will operate in practice.

Consider, for instance, President Franklin Roosevelt's creation of the Works Progress Administration (WPA). In 1935, Congress passed the Emergency Relief Appropriations Act, which broadly delegated power and some funds to the president "to increase employment by providing useful projects."[39] Roosevelt then issued an executive order creating the WPA, and, according to Roosevelt's speechwriter and confidante Robert Sherwood, "Roosevelt suggested that it would be mainly a 'bookkeeping' organization."[40] Slipped into the executive order was a line that the WPA would "recommend and carry on small useful projects designed to assure a maximum of employment in all localities."[41] As Sherwood later wrote about this innocuous-sounding phrase:

> That was a loophole for [WPA administrator Harry] Hopkins—and Roosevelt was well aware of it—which assumed continental proportions. Those "small projects" represented an expenditure eventually of over ten billion dollars [exceeding $220 billion in 2025 dollars]. . . . In the first three years of this program something like a quarter of a million individual projects [were commenced]. . . . WPA was by all odds the biggest of the Federal employers and spenders.[42]

Consider also the creation of concentration camps for allegedly untrustworthy residents and citizens of Japanese descent—so-called Japanese internment—in the Western United States during World War II. Here is the operative language in Roosevelt's February 19, 1942, executive order, largely ratified and reproduced in legislation weeks later:

> I hereby authorize and direct the Secretary of War, and the Military Commanders whom he may from time to time designate, whenever he or any designated Commander deems such action necessary or desirable, to prescribe military areas in such places and of such extent as he or the appropriate Military Commander may determine, from which any or all persons may be excluded.[43]

Most people and members of Congress probably envisioned a process resembling the attorney general's practice of creating exclusion zones to the public around airports, dams, power plants, pumping stations, and military installations. "In most cases the areas were small, usually circles of 1,000 feet or rectangles of several city blocks."[44] So it was difficult to anticipate the unprecedented actions this order authorized—that the whole Western United States would be declared a "military area" and that residents with Japanese ancestry, including some

70,000 American citizens, would be compelled to leave their homes and live in a system of concentration camps for three years.[45]

The War Department even considered the mass deportation of Americans and residents with German and Italian ancestry to concentration camps on the East Coast as falling within the purpose of the executive order.[46] President Roosevelt demurred on this proposal for unclear reasons,[47] though he did authorize the military to deport thousands of residents of German and Italian descent, including some American citizens, to concentration camps.[48] Thousands more were required to self-deport from coastal areas.[49]

Even in this egregious case of arbitrary lawmaking via executive order, courts blessed the assertion of executive power. An American of Japanese descent who refused to comply with the deportation orders was convicted under the federal law passed by Congress that ratified Executive Order 9066. He challenged the law as an unconstitutional delegation of legislative power to the executive and to the military.[50] His case, *Hirabayashi v. United States*, reached the Supreme Court in 1943. In *Hirabayashi*, the Court tersely held that the delegation (such as it was) to the president was a permissible "emergency war measure."[51] Similarly, the next year the Supreme Court sustained the internal deportation of Americans in *Korematsu v. United States* because "the military urgency of the situation demanded" it.[52]

In the 1970s, Congress attempted to limit the president's broad emergency powers to his response to "unusual and extraordinary" threats to America and the government's foreign policy.[53] While that sounds like a limit on the president's power, presidents have long interpreted "emergency" quite loosely.[54] Today, America is still under several emergencies. It appears some national emergencies are perpetual because they reference unyielding realities, like the existence of biological and nuclear weapons.[55] Some national emergencies are quite dubious, like those that characterize the internal politics of and conflicts within tiny nations and minor powers as "constitut[ing] an unusual and extraordinary threat to the national security and foreign policy of the United States."[56] Furthermore, government officials often cite amorphous national security interests to justify the warrantless collection of millions of Americans' digital communications[57] and brutal economic sanctions against many countries.[58] Presidents and their legal advisers also assert broad and rarely used powers, like the power to search Americans' homes without a warrant when searching for "foreign intelligence."[59] This legal dark matter of executive powers that functions as lawmaking power shows no sign of abatement, 90 years after President Franklin Roosevelt and a quiescent Congress introduced it.

Conclusion

The Framers of the Constitution did not anticipate that Congress would surrender its constitutional lawmaking powers to the president—and then refuse to reclaim them. Nor could they have foreseen the extreme deference that courts would show to Congress and to the president. Furthermore, Congress and the courts have not consistently defended against executive assertions of unenumerated powers. As a result, there is a one-way ratchet effect of presidential declarations of national emergencies, which give shape to the "dark matter" of latent federal powers.[60] Presidents and Congress have immense incentives to keep Americans in a perpetual, low-grade, president-ordained state of emergency. Until there is a revolution in jurisprudence or politics, the president's and Congress's latent emergency powers won't recede to the limits the Founders envisioned.

Notes

1. See *Ex parte Merryman*, 17 F. Cas. 144, 148 (C.C.D. Md. 1861).
2. Exec. Order No. 9981, 13 Fed. Reg. 4313 (July 28, 1948).
3. Exec. Order No. 9066 (Feb. 19, 1942). See also The Commission on Wartime Relocation and Internment of Civilians, *Personal Justice Denied* (US Government Printing Office, 1983).
4. Exec. Order No. 13333, 3 C.F.R. 200 (1981), amended by Exec. Order No. 13284, 3 C.F.R. 161 (2003); Exec. Order No. 13355, 3 C.F.R. 218 (2004), and Exec. Order No. 13470, 3 C.F.R. 218 (2008).
5. US Const. art. I, § 1.
6. US Const. art. II, § 3.
7. Kenneth R. Mayer, *With the Stroke of a Pen: Executive Orders and Presidential Power* (Princeton University Press, 2001), p. 34. Today, executive orders are typically published in the *Federal Register* but, given the slipperiness of the concept, "an executive order is whatever the president chooses to call by that name."
8. See Erica Newland, "Executive Orders in Court," *Yale Law Journal* 124, no. 6 (2015): 2031–32. While executive orders can impose legal obligations on

government employees and the public, "executive orders without specific foundation in congressional action are not judicially enforceable in private civil suits." In *Re Surface Mining Regulation Litigation*, 627 F.2d 1346, 1357 (DC Cir. 1980). See also Newland, "Executive Orders in Court," pp. 2075–79.

9. Truman may have followed the example of his predecessor, Franklin Roosevelt, who seized at least two aviation plants (in peacetime) in Exec. Order No. 8773, 6 Fed. Reg. 2777 (June 9, 1941) (seizure of North American Aviation, Inc.); Exec. Order No. 8928 (Oct. 30, 1941) (seizure of Air Associates, Inc.).

10. *Youngstown Sheet & Tube Co. v. Sawyer*, 343 US 579, 585 (1952).

11. Nineteenth-century courts slowly blessed the assertion of inherent but unenumerated executive powers. For instance, in the 1862 *Prize Cases* the Supreme Court held, in a 5-4 opinion, that President Lincoln was permitted to initiate an act of war—a blockade of Confederate ports—even though Congress had not declared war. The Court did not cite constitutional principles but, rather, the international law of war to uphold the president's authority. *Prize Cases*, 67 US 635, 671 (1862) ("[W]e are of the opinion that the President had a right, jure belli [trans. "law of war"], to institute a blockade of ports in possession of the States in rebellion.")

12. Decades ago, former Secretary of the Interior Harold L. Ickes estimated the number of unnumbered executive orders as 15,000, while others placed the figure as high as 50,000. House Committee on Government Operations, 85th Cong., 1st Sess., *Executive Orders and Proclamations: A Study of a Use of Presidential Powers* (US Government Printing Office, 1957), p. 37.

13. Exec. Order (April 25, 1861).

14. Exec. Order (April 27, 1861).

15. Authorizing General Winfield Scott to Suspend the Writ of *Habeas Corpus*, Exec. Order (July 2, 1861); Suspension of the Writ of Habeas Corpus, Exec. Order (Oct. 14, 1861).

16. Congressional Research Service, *Executive Orders and Proclamations*, CRS-4 (US Government Printing Office, March 9, 1999).

17. House Committee on Government Operations, *Executive Orders and Proclamations*, p. 35.

18. See, e.g., Exec. Order (July 2, 1888).

19. See Louis Fisher, *Constitutional Conflicts Between Congress and the President*, 4th ed., rev. ed. (University Press of Kansas, 1997), p. 110.

20. House Committee on Government Operations, *Executive Orders and Proclamations*, p. 36.

21. *Home Building & Loan Assn. v. Blaisdell*, 290 US 398, 426 (1934).

22. See search results for executive orders declaring a national emergency, The American Presidency Project, U.C. Santa Barbara, accessed April 16, 2025.

23. Presidential Proclamation No. 2039, reprinted in 48 Stat. 1691 (1933).

24. 50 U.S.C., Ch. 106, § 5(b), 40 Stat. 411 (1917). See also *Stoehr v. Wallace*, 255 US 239, 242 (1921). ("The Trading with the Enemy Act . . . is strictly a war measure.")

25. George Selgin, "The New Deal and Recovery, Part 6: The National Bank Holiday," *Cato at Liberty* (blog), Cato Institute, July 28, 2020.

26. See Mary M. C. Bowman, "Presidential Emergency Powers Related to International Economic Transactions," *Vanderbilt Law Review* 11, no. 3 (1978): 518n27.

27. Emergency Banking Relief Act of 1933, ch. 1, § 2, 48 Stat. 1.

28. Edward S. Miller, *Bankrupting the Enemy: The U.S. Financial Siege of Japan Before Pearl Harbor* (Naval Institute Press, 2007), pp. 5–6.

29. Another possible example of the cascading effect of executive orders is that in July 1941, during peacetime, President Roosevelt issued an executive order to apply the Trading with the Enemy Act to sanction Japan. Amendment of Executive Order No. 8389 of April 10, 1940, as amended, Exec. Order 8832 (July 31, 1941). In September, the general counsel for the Treasury Department boasted that the administration had "changed the emphasis of freezing control from a defensive weapon . . . to a frankly aggressive weapon against the Axis." As a result, "the economy of Japan has suffered a profound shock." Edward H. Foley, Jr., general counsel for the Treasury Department, Freezing Control as a Weapon of Economic Defense, address delivered before the Committee on Insurance Law, American Bar Association, Sept. 29, 1941, reprinted in New York Federal Reserve Bank Circular, Nov. 7, 1941.

30. Reopening Banks, Exec. Order No. 6073 (1933).

31. Forbidding the Hoarding of Gold Coin, Gold Bullion and Gold Certificates, Exec. Order No. 6102 (1933).

32. Forbidding the Hoarding of Gold Coin, Gold Bullion and Gold Certificates, Exec. Order No. 6102, Sec. 9 (1933).

33. Agricultural Adjustment Act of 1933, Pub. L. No. 73-10, 48 Stat. 31 (granting, for instance, the agriculture secretary power to pay farmers "such amounts as the Secretary deems fair and reasonable" to not produce).

34. Act of March 3, 1933, Pub. L. No. 428, 47 Stat. 1517.

35. National Industry Recovery Act of 1933, Pub. L. No. 73-67, 48 Stat. 195 (granting, for instance, the president power to impose a compulsory "code of fair competition" on any "trade or industry or subdivision thereof").

36. Exec. Order No. 8773, 6 Fed. Reg. 2777 (1941) (seizing aviation plant). The president sent 2,500 Army troops to seize the plant. Foster Hailey, "Bayonets on Coast: Work on War Planes Resumes as Pickets Yield to 2,500 Soldiers," *New York Times*, June 10, 1941, p. 1. After seizing the plant, Roosevelt administration officials ordered that remaining strikers lose their draft deferments and be subjected to compelled military service. Charles Hurd, "Draft Deferment Ends for Strikers," *New York Times*, June 10, 1941, p. 1.

37. Withdrawing Public Lands for Use of the War Department as a Demolition and Practice Bombing Range, Exec. Order 8755 (May 16, 1941).

38. Regulating Transactions in Foreign Exchange and Foreign-Owned Property, Providing for the Reporting of All Foreign-Owned Property, and Related Matters, Exec. Order No. 8785 (June 14, 1941).

39. Act of April 8, 1935, Pub. L. 74-28, 49 Stat. 113.

40. Robert E. Sherwood, *Roosevelt and Hopkins: An Intimate History* (Harper & Brothers, 1948), p. 69.

41. Establishing the Division of Applications and Information, the Advisory Committee on Allotments, the Works Progress Administration, and for Other Purposes, Exec. Order No. 7034 (May 6, 1935).

42. Sherwood, *Roosevelt and Hopkins*, pp. 69–70.

43. Act of March 21, 1942, Pub. L. 503, 56 Stat. 173.

44. The Commission on Wartime Relocation and Internment of Civilians, *Personal Justice Denied*, p. 72.

45. *Korematsu v. United States*, 323 US 214, 242 (1944) (Murphy, J., dissenting) (noting the number of American citizens in camps). In the weeks between Roosevelt's order and Congress's ratification of the order, there were signals that the administration held an expansive view of its relocation authority. A March 2, 1942, proclamation and press release made much of the West Coast a "military area" and made clear that Americans with Japanese ancestry would be forced to relocate from much of the West Coast. Proclamation No. 1 of March 2, 1942 (Lieut. Gen. DeWitt). DeWitt's later proclamations made it a crime for Americans of Japanese ancestry to possess firearms. See Proclamation No. 3 of March 24, 1942 (Lieut. Gen. DeWitt).

46. The Commission on Wartime Relocation and Internment of Civilians, *Personal Justice Denied*, p. 85.

47. The Commission on Wartime Relocation and Internment of Civilians, *Personal Justice Denied*, p. 85.

48. See, e.g., Christopher Tremoglie, "80 Years Later, Most Unaware of Italian and German Internment Camps in the US," *Washington Examiner*, February 18, 2022. Tremoglie also discusses the smaller numbers of people of Czech, Romanian, Bulgarian, and Hungarian descent also deported to camps. See also Wartime Violation of Italian American Civil Liberties Act, Pub. L. 106-451 (2000) (congressional finding that "During World War II thousands of Italian American immigrants were arrested, and hundreds were interned in military camps").

49. Wartime Violation of Italian American Civil Liberties Act, Pub. L. 106-451 (2000) (congressional finding that "During World War II more than 10,000 Italian Americans living on the West Coast were forced to leave their homes and prohibited from entering coastal zones").

50. *Hirabayashi v. United States*, 320 US 81, 89 (1943).

51. *Hirabayashi v. United States*, 320 US 81, 92 (1943).

52. *Korematsu v. United States*, 323 US 214, 223 (1944). In 2018, the Supreme Court repudiated and overruled *Korematsu*, stating: "The forcible relocation of U.S. citizens to concentration camps, solely and explicitly on the basis of race, is objectively unlawful and outside the scope of Presidential authority." *Trump v. Hawaii*, 585 US 667 (2018).

53. See 50 U.S.C. § 1701.

54. For instance, a judge recently asked a Trump administration lawyer for a limiting principle for "unusual and extraordinary" national threats. The government was unable to offer one: Judge Restani asked whether a national peanut butter shortage might constitute an "unusual and extraordinary threat." The administration replied, "it probably depends." Oral Argument at 1:09:25, *V.O.S. Selections, Inc. v. Trump*, No. 1:25-cv-00066 (Court of International Trade, May 13, 2025).

55. Proliferation of Weapons of Mass Destruction, Exec. Order No. 12938 (November 14, 1994).

56. See, e.g., Blocking Property of Certain Persons Contributing to the Situation in Nicaragua, Exec. Order No. 13851 (November 27, 2018) (people who "have directly or indirectly engaged or attempted to engage in . . . actions or policies that undermine democratic processes or institutions in Nicaragua"); Blocking Property of Certain Persons Contributing to the Conflict in Cote d'Ivoire, Exec. Order No. 13396 (Feb. 7, 2006) (people "publicly incited violence and hatred" in

Cote d'Ivoire); Blocking Property of Persons Who Threaten International Stabilization Efforts in the Western Balkans, Exec. Order No. 13219 (June 26, 2001) (people "engaged in, or . . . support[ed]" extremist violence in the Balkans); Blocking Property of Certain Persons Contributing to the Situation in Ukraine, Exec. Order No. 13660 (March 6, 2014) (people "undermined democratic processes and institutions" in Ukraine).

57. Exec. Order No. 12333 (December 4, 1981) amended by Exec. Order No. 13284, 3 C.F.R. 161 (2003); Exec. Order No. 13355, 3 C.F.R. 218 (2004), and Exec. Order No. 13470, 3 C.F.R. 218 (2008).

58. Generally, sanctions against a nation's leaders do not achieve their intended effects and harm many innocent people. See Richard Hanania, "Ineffective, Immoral, Politically Convenient: America's Overreliance on Economic Sanctions and What to Do About It," Cato Institute Policy Analysis no. 884, February 18, 2020.

59. It is the Department of Justice's position that "the President has inherent authority under the Constitution to conduct foreign intelligence searches of the private homes of U.S. citizens in the United States without a warrant." Prepared statement of Honorable Alberto R. Gonzales, attorney general of the United States, February 6, 2006 (quoting and citing affirmative testimony to Congress from President Clinton's Deputy Attorney General Jamie Gorelick). Given the broad definition of "foreign intelligence," tens of millions of American homes are potentially subject to warrantless entry and search. See, e.g., 50 USC § 3003 (defining "foreign intelligence" merely as "information relating to the capabilities, intentions, or activities of . . . foreign persons").

60. Robert Higgs, for instance, has discussed the ratchet effect of government powers during crisis: "When crisis provoked an extension of governmental powers, the new powers in a fundamental sense never could be merely transitory." Robert Higgs, *Crisis and Leviathan* (Independent Institute, 2012), chap. 4.

ABOUT THE EDITOR

THOMAS A. BERRY is the director of the Cato Institute's Robert A. Levy Center for Constitutional Studies and editor in chief of the *Cato Supreme Court Review.* Before joining Cato, he was an attorney at the Pacific Legal Foundation and clerked for Judge E. Grady Jolly of the US Court of Appeals for the Fifth Circuit. Berry's areas of interest include the separation of powers, executive branch appointments, and First Amendment freedom of speech. Berry holds a JD from Stanford Law School, where he was a senior editor on the *Stanford Law & Policy Review* and a Bradley Fellow in the Stanford Constitutional Law Center. He graduated with a BA in liberal arts from St. John's College, Santa Fe.

ABOUT THE CONTRIBUTORS

DAVID BIER is director of immigration studies and occupies The Selz Foundation Chair in Immigration Policy at the Cato Institute. He is an expert on legal immigration, border security, and interior enforcement. Bier's work has appeared in the *New York Times*, the *Washington Post*, *USA Today*, and many other print and online publications. The US Supreme Court and multiple federal appeals courts have cited his research and writing. Bier has testified before House and Senate committees on several occasions. From 2013 to 2015, Bier drafted immigration legislation as a senior policy adviser for then-Representative Raúl Labrador (R-ID), then a member and later the chair of the House Judiciary Committee's Subcommittee on Immigration and Border Security.

BRANDAN P. BUCK is a research fellow in foreign policy studies at the Cato Institute. He is a historian specializing in domestic opposition to US foreign policy in the 20th century, postwar conservatism, and the national security state. His research covers the impact of an activist foreign policy on American society and civil liberties, the history of US strategic thinking and its implications for contemporary politics, and the politics of foreign policy. Buck's work has appeared in scholarly journals and popular outlets, including the *International History Review*, *Responsible Statecraft*, *The American Conservative*, *Reason*, *Strategy Bridge*, Antiwar.com, and the Libertarian Institute.

DOUGLAS A. IRWIN is John French Professor of Economics at Dartmouth College. He is the author of *Clashing over Commerce: A History of US Trade Policy* (University of Chicago Press, 2017), which was selected by *The Economist* and *Foreign Affairs* as one of the best books of the year. He is also the author of *Free Trade Under Fire*, 5th ed. (Princeton University Press, 2020); *Trade Policy Disaster: Lessons from the 1930s* (MIT Press, 2012); *Peddling Protectionism: Smoot-Hawley and the Great Depression* (Princeton University Press, 2011); *The Genesis of the GATT* (Cambridge University Press, April 2008), with Petros Mavroidis and Alan Sykes; and *Against the Tide: An Intellectual History of Free Trade* (Princeton University Press, 1996), along with many articles on trade policy and economic history. He is a research associate at the National Bureau of Economic Research and a nonresident senior fellow at the Peterson Institute for International Economics. He worked on trade policy issues for President Ronald Reagan's Council of Economic Advisers and for the Federal Reserve Board of Governors.

JOSHUA LOUCKS is a former research associate at the Cato Institute, where he specialized in analyzing the economic and budgetary effects of taxation, energy policy, and environmental regulation. Before joining Cato, he was an MA Fellow for the Mercatus Center at George Mason University. Loucks holds a BA in political science from Virginia Polytechnic Institute and State University and an MA in economics from George Mason University.

ADAM N. MICHEL is director of tax policy studies at the Cato Institute, where he focuses on analyzing the economic and budgetary effects of taxation in the United States. Before joining Cato, Michel served as deputy staff director at the US Congress Joint Economic Committee, where he helped lead Senator Mike Lee's (R-UT) Social Capital Project, organized congressional hearings, and produced research on a wide array of current economic topics. Michel's work has been widely published and quoted in the *Wall Street Journal*, the *New York Times*, the *Washington Post*, and elsewhere. He has also appeared on Fox News, CNN, and CNBC to discuss tax policy and its economic effects. His scholarly work has been published in *Public Budgeting & Finance* and *Tax Notes*, as well as in numerous book chapters.

CLARK NEILY is senior vice president for legal studies at the Cato Institute. His areas of interest include constitutional law, overcriminalization, coercive plea bargaining, police accountability, and gun rights. Before joining Cato in 2017, Neily was a senior attorney and constitutional litigator at the Institute for Justice and director of its Center for Judicial Engagement. Neily is the author of *Terms of Engagement: How Our Courts Should Enforce the Constitution's Promise of Limited Government*. He also contributed a chapter to Libertarianism.org's book, *Visions of Liberty*.

ROGER PILON is a senior fellow in the Cato Institute's Center for Constitutional Studies, which he founded in 1989 and directed until 2019; the inaugural holder emeritus of Cato's B. Kenneth Simon Chair in Constitutional Studies, Cato's first endowed chair, established in 1998; and the publisher emeritus of the *Cato Supreme Court Review*, which he founded in 2001. He was also appointed as Cato's vice president for legal affairs in 1999. His writings have appeared in the *Wall Street Journal*, the *Washington Post*, the *New York Times*, the *Los Angeles Times*, the *Legal Times* (now part of the Law.com network), the *National Law Journal*, the *Harvard Journal of Law & Public Policy*, the *Stanford Law & Policy Review*, and elsewhere. He has appeared on ABC's *Nightline*, CBS's *60 Minutes II*, Fox News, NPR, CNN, MSNBC, CNBC, C-SPAN, and other media.

BRENT SKORUP is a legal fellow in the Cato Institute's Robert A. Levy Center for Constitutional Studies. Before joining Cato, he was a senior research fellow at the Mercatus Center at George Mason University and a legal clerk at the Federal Communications Commission's Wireless Telecommunications Bureau and Office of General Counsel and at the Energy and Commerce Committee in the US House of Representatives. His research areas include free speech, technology law, Fourth Amendment protections, regulation, and property law. Skorup has had his work published in economics and law journals, as well as in popular media outlets such as the *Wall Street Journal*, the *New York Times*, Bloomberg Law, Reuters, and *WIRED*. He has appeared as a TV and radio interview guest for news outlets such as C-SPAN, NPR, CBS News, ABC News, and CNBC Asia.

ABOUT THE CATO INSTITUTE

Founded in 1977, the Cato Institute is a public policy research foundation dedicated to broadening the parameters of policy debate to allow consideration of more options that are consistent with the traditional American principles of limited government, individual liberty, and peace. To that end, the Institute strives to achieve greater involvement of the intelligent, concerned lay public in questions of policy and the proper role of government.

The Institute is named for *Cato's Letters*, libertarian pamphlets that were widely read in the American Colonies in the early 18th century and that played a major role in laying the philosophical foundation for the American Revolution.

Despite the achievement of the nation's Founders, today virtually no aspect of life is free from government encroachment. A pervasive intolerance for individual rights is shown by government's arbitrary intrusions into private economic transactions and its disregard for civil liberties.

To counter that trend, the Cato Institute undertakes an extensive publications program that addresses the complete spectrum of policy issues. Books, monographs, and shorter studies are commissioned to examine the federal budget, Social Security, regulation, military spending, international trade, and myriad other issues.

In order to maintain its independence, the Cato Institute accepts no government funding. Contributions are received from foundations, corporations, and individuals, and other revenue is generated from the sale of publications. The Institute is a nonprofit, tax-exempt, educational foundation under Section 501(c)3 of the Internal Revenue Code.

CATO INSTITUTE
1000 Massachusetts Ave. NW
Washington, D.C. 20001
www.cato.org